EVIDENCE FROM BEYOND

THE REVEREND A. D. MATTSON, S. T. D.
1895–1970

EVIDENCE
from BEYOND

An Insider's Guide
to the Wonders of Heaven—
and Life in the New Millennium

More After-Death Communications
Received from Theologian
A.D. MATTSON

Through Clairvoyant
MARGARET FLAVELL

EDITED BY
RUTH MATTSON TAYLOR

B

BRETT BOOKS, INC.
BROOKLYN, NEW YORK

Published in the United States of America by Brett Books, Inc., P.O. Box 290-637, Brooklyn, New York 11229-0637.

All Scripture quotations are taken from the HOLY BIBLE, NEW INTERNATIONAL VERSION, Copyright © 1973, 1978, 1984 by International Bible Society. Used by permission of Zondervan Publishing House.

Library of Congress Cataloging-in-Publication Data
Mattson, A. D. (Alvin Daniel), 1895-1970 (Spirit)
    Evidence from beyond : an insider's guide to the wonders of heaven—and life in the new millennium : more after-death communications received from theologian A.D. Mattson, through clairvoyant Margaret Flavell / edited by Ruth Mattson Taylor. — 1st ed.
      p.   cm.
    Includes bibliographical references (p.   ).
    ISBN 0-9636620-5-8
    1. Spirit writings.   I. Flavell, Margaret.   II. Taylor, Ruth Mattson.   III. Title.
BF1301.M43 1999
133.9'3—DC21   99-22754

First Edition
Manufactured in the United States of America
Printed on acid-free paper

99 00 01 02 03 04 05   10 9 8 7 6 5 4 3 2 1

Book design by C. Linda Dingler

To Margaret Flavell,
who opened the gate for me
to a whole new dimension of existence

The wise of all the earth have said in their hearts always: "God is, and there is none beside Him"; and the fools of all the earth have said in their hearts always: "I am, and there is none beside me."

JOHN RUSKIN

CONTENTS

CONTENTS

ACKNOWLEDGMENTS

THE ADVANCE READERS of this book have mentioned its easy-flowing and reader-friendly style. Credit for this must go to the reformatting and fine-tuning of my original manuscript by my editor and publisher, Barbara Brett. I am deeply grateful for her editorial skill and her diligent help in presenting A.D.'s material to the readers of this book.

I also want to express my thanks to author Hy Brett, Barbara's husband, for his support and help in many ways.

My thanks are also given to the Reverend Eric J. Gustavson, former student of A.D. Mattson, for his permission to quote from his tribute to A.D. on the occasion of A.D.'s retirement, and to Dr. Sally Feather of the Rhine Research Center for permission to quote from J.B. Rhine's book *New World of the Mind*.

I must also express my sincere appreciation to the gracious and busy people who gave of their time to do an advance reading of the manuscript and whose overwhelming, positive response reinforced my own conviction of the importance of A.D.'s message for our world today. My thanks for this goes to: the Reverend Elizabeth W. Fenske,

Ph.D., Executive Director of Spiritual Frontiers Fellowship International; to Elda Hartley, President of Hartley Film Foundation and Life Director of the Institute of Noetic Sciences; to Juliet Hollister, founder of The Temple of Understanding; to John F. Miller III, Ph.D., President of the Academy of Religion and Psychical Research; to the Reverend John H. Nasstrom, Ph.D., retired Lutheran pastor and church executive, and former student of A.D. Mattson; to the Right Reverend Bennett J. Sims, Bishop Emeritus of the Episcopal Diocese of Atlanta, and founder and president of the Institute for Servant Leadership; to Frank Tribbe, Editor of *Spiritual Frontiers Journal;* and to Claire Walker, Ph.D., Editor of *Reflections of a Theosophist.*

Thanks must also be given to the Reverend William H. Gentz, who provided very early editorial guidance, and who encouraged me to include some of my own personal paranormal experiences in this book.

R.M.T.

South Portland, ME

PROLOGUE

PREPARING FOR
THE JOURNEY

I will instruct you and teach you in the way you should go;
I will counsel you and watch over you.

PSALMS 32:8

SOMETHING STRANGE HAPPENED when I was a little girl. I lived with my parents in the Lutheran parsonage at St. James, Minnesota, and one autumn night after a fresh snowfall, our doorbell rang at three o'clock in the morning. My father, the Reverend A.D. Mattson, went down to open the door. He found no one there, and there were no footprints in the newly fallen snow. One could conjecture either that my father had imagined hearing the doorbell, or that he had dreamed it. But both my mother and a young schoolteacher who roomed at the parsonage had also heard the bell.

The next morning, when the three of them were having breakfast together, the phone rang. The phone call was from my father's sister, Lydia, who was a nurse at the Lutheran hospital in Moline, Illinois. Lydia was calling to tell us that my father's Aunt Amanda had died during the night, at around three o'clock in the morning.

Some parapsychologists would explain the simultaneous ringing of the parsonage doorbell and the death of Amanda as a physical manifestation by Amanda's spirit to tell her nephew that she had died. Such physical manifestations by spirit personalities are categorized as telekinesis, and in paranormal literature there are many references to such happenings. Over the years, similar occurrences at the deaths of several of my mother's relatives had led us to accept these phenomena as a normal part of life.

My father had an active interest in parapsychology throughout his lifetime, and he was exposed to scientific investigation of these areas of study when he was doing postgraduate work at Yale Divinity School in 1929. Some of the professors there were studying the work of the famous medium Margery in Boston, as well as other paranormal phenomena. On numerous occasions, my father had said that when he died, he would certainly attempt to communicate with us.

Affectionately known as "A.D." to hundreds of former students, colleagues, and friends, my father, Lutheran theologian Alvin Daniel Mattson, S.T.D., died on October 19, 1970. His communication from Beyond began in 1971. Although not as frequent as it was in the first few years after his death, his contact has continued to the present time.

Not quite five months after A.D. died, Margaret Flavell, a close friend from London, was visiting us. She is one of the most respected clairvoyants in England and has a remarkable record of accomplishments in the field of psychic communication. On the morning of March 2, 1971, we decided to see if we could get in touch with A.D. in the world beyond and to tape-record our attempt. We had expected to make contact with him and to get evidence that he does survive, but little did we expect the quantity and quality of very significant communication and information that we received. From March 1971 through October 1973 we received fifty-five communications, amounting to over five hundred legal-sized pages of typed transcripts. Much of that material was personal for the immediate family, but we extracted information we felt would be of interest to the general reader and presented it in *Witness from Beyond*, first published by Hawthorn Books in 1975. That book is now regarded as a classic on inter-life communication by experts in parapsychology.

Since that time, to eliminate the tedious process of transcribing the tape recordings, Margaret has written down most of the communications. On some occasions, though, we still use the tape recorder.

There are many theories about the sources of material brought through to us by mediums. Some suggest that mediums tap knowledge from their own "higher selves," or tap a "world mind-pool of knowledge," or tap a "universal mind," or have telepathic reception from a sitter or direct communication from a discarnate (no longer living) person. Margaret and I are not attempting to prove or disprove any of these theories. We are simply presenting what has been a most relevant experience for us. Readers will have to draw their own conclusions after analyzing the contents.

A sensing of truth in mystical areas often comes by direct insight, as indeed does faith in God. From what we have experienced, I am firmly convinced that A.D. survives, and that, with the help of others in the realm beyond, he has been given the privilege and opportunity to communicate to us a vision of that realm, in the hope that it will give more meaning to our lives on earth.

The fact that Margaret Flavell and A.D. never met while he was on earth makes the evidential material of the communications, as well as the nuances of A.D.'s personality that come through, all the more significant. "Evidential" material is that which gives substantiation to the identity of A.D. as the communicator from Beyond. There is strong evidence that A.D. is the communicator, and it is presented in the chapter "Confirmation from Beyond" in Part One.

We cannot hope to grasp fully some of the material. Dealing with concepts of the realm beyond, it comes from a sphere of experience that is not yet ours. Every reader will have to interpret and accept according to his or her own understanding. For those unfamiliar with parapsychology, we have included a suggested bibliography for additional reading. In addition, a glossary with simple definitions is also provided at the end of the book.

Through the magnificent journey that begins on the following pages, we hope that the reader will come to an inner state of knowing that death is but a transition, a door, to another dimension of living, one with continued growth and challenges. This can make the living of every single day on earth an exciting, new adventure—a journey of its own, to be embarked on in faith, not fear.

PART ONE

THE PILGRIMS

A.D., THE COMMUNICATOR

I sought the Lord and he answered me;
he delivered me from all my fears.
PSALMS 34:4

THE REVEREND ALVIN DANIEL MATTSON, S.T.D., affectionately known as "A.D.," was constantly leading the way into new frontiers. He was a pioneer among the clergymen who sought to awaken the organized church to its responsibilities in the area of social justice. In the mid-1960s one of his former students wrote a tribute to him on the occasion of his retirement from teaching:

> Here is a man who cannot be measured by the standards by which we judge just ordinary men. For when God put his hand on [A.D.'s] shoulder, He really had a man for a special mission in His church, physically and courageously strong, a man with a good mind and a compassionate heart.
>
> As a teacher, [A.D.] taught us a living, exciting, dynamic and relevant Gospel. He introduced us to the prophets, he took us by the hand and led us into those areas of life that the Church had so long neglected, and on every step of the way his faith, his love for his fellowmen and his courage were demonstrated.

The present generation of students, accustomed to reading the pronouncements of the Church on civil rights, open occupancy and related social concerns, will never know, unless we tell them so, how responsible he is for the Church's present stand on social justice. It is his students, who, having caught his prophetic spirit and loving concern for the economically and socially disinherited, are today standing in picket lines, going on freedom marches, integrating their churches and writing the social pronouncements of their churches. This reflects the fact that "A.D." was not only a prophet, but a great teacher. Perhaps no teacher in the history of Augustana Seminary has made so great an impact on so many for so great a cause as has our beloved teacher.

The entire church, the personal life of hundreds of students, the lives of countless men and women in the hard places of life have been enriched by the life, the teachings, the courage and the love of A.D. Mattson, a man's man and a man of God.[1]

A.D. was a man for all people. He had a deep love and compassion for all humanity, and was as much at home with the farmer and the laborer as he was with the theologian.

A.D.'s appreciation of the people who farm our land and provide our food stemmed from the fact that he was the son of a minister who served in primarily rural areas. His growing-up years gave him an intimate knowledge of the life and problems of the farmer. His understanding was deepened by his own early pastoral ministry in rural parishes in Minnesota. His prophetic concern for the ecological stewardship of our earth grew out of these experiences.

In his teens, A.D. worked on railroad labor gangs and on factory assembly lines to earn money for his education. He learned firsthand what hard labor was, and his concern throughout his life for fair wages and proper working conditions for all stemmed from his own personal experience. For more than eighteen years he was Protestant chaplain of the Quad-City Federation of Labor in Illinois, and he counted thousands of workers among his friends. He was often called on by both management and labor to mediate their differences, and in 1950 he was employed by the United States Department of State to make a special study of the labor conditions in postwar Germany. He conducted seminars on industry and labor at the Augustana Seminary, and personally exposed his students to these areas, which had been long neglected by the church. He and his students often walked the picket lines with strikers, if they felt their cause was just. On the other hand, if A.D. felt that labor was unreasonable in its actions or demands, he did not hesitate to say so.

He traveled widely to study the plight of the underprivileged in this country, in Mexico, and in Europe, and he made his students aware of many of the social problems in our nation and the world. The fight against racism, including fair housing and equal job opportunities; the struggle of John L. Lewis against the near-serfdom of miners; the plight of the sharecroppers in the South; the support of conscientious objectors in the struggle against war; concern for ecological stewardship of the earth—these were but a few of his deep concerns.

"Thy kingdom come. Thy will be done..." was for A.D. a foundation for his life. He believed that every person born to this world, regardless of race, creed, or color, has a right to develop to his or her fullest potential. Environmental conditions were extremely important to him. A.D. realized that a starving man living in squalor cannot develop fully, nor can he experience the "shalom," the peace and wholeness, that is his birthright. The sacredness of human life and the biblical command that we are our brother's keeper were the watchwords of A.D.'s life and faith. Wherever profit and greed took precedence over human well-being, A.D., standing firmly on the Scriptures, voiced God's condemnation.

The Reverend Allen C. Nelson, a former student who preached his funeral sermon, said: "Of A.D. it surely can be said: he didn't preach the gospel—he was the gospel!"

During his many years of seminary teaching, few people were aware of A.D.'s deep interest in parapsychology. A.D. was known as a Christian ethicist and a champion for social justice and reform, and he didn't publicly stress his parapsychological interests. For him, survival after death was a matter of deep, personal faith. But when a student questioned the probability of survival after death or showed an interest in parapsychology, A.D. was ready to counsel that student and suggest material for study.

A.D. blazed new trails when he was on earth. He now continues to blaze new trails of understanding from Beyond.

CONFIRMATION
FROM BEYOND

I am fully convinced that the soul is indestructible, and that its activity will continue through eternity. It is like the sun, which, to our eyes, seems to set in night; but it has in reality only gone to diffuse its light elsewhere.

GOETHE

"EVIDENTIAL" MATERIAL GIVES confirmation to the identity of the unseen communicator. Based on situation verification and the nuances of A.D.'s personality that come through the taped communications, there is strong evidence that A.D. is indeed the communicator who is speaking to us from Beyond. These same facts are presented in *Witness from Beyond*, but they are essential to assure new friends that it is indeed A.D. who is the communicator, and to recall these incidents for old friends.

After the first group of sittings, intentional evidential material was not given too frequently. A.D. pointed out that he already had given enough such information to assure us of his identity. He told us that he did not intend to deplete his mind-directive power and stored energy by continually giving such material. Rather, his purpose is to bring through information that will extend our vision and be of value to our living experience here on earth. (On occasion he has stated that his mind-directive "current" was running out, and we have had to break the session for a time, indicating that the energy power with which the invisibles communicate is not unlimited.)

The following sections present some of the significant evidential material. Evidential accounts of a very personal nature pertaining to the immediate family are not included.

LIFE'S DISCIPLINES

In the first sitting on March 2, 1971, A.D. spoke about the disciplines of life: "So many people have the feeling that they must work according to the way *they* feel. They say, 'Lord, use us,' but they don't want to be garbagemen or they don't want to be a lot of things which God might want them to be." And humorously he continued, "They might have to cook, even. That, too, is a discipline. When I could accept it as a discipline and get my juicer going, then I could enjoy even that.

"This is something that has to be taught to people—that the disciplines of life are those that are imposed by the surroundings and the obligations to society. God doesn't impose the disciplines. He gives us perfect freedom in spirit. It is we who have to put our disciplines on ourselves."

That statement contains several very evidential points. When on earth, A.D. constantly stressed the sacredness of human life and the importance of each person to the total scheme of things. This applied also to the various vocations people have. He often would illustrate this to us by pointing out that all honest, contributing labor, from that of the *garbageman* to that of the *academician*, is essential to life and of equal worth in the sight of God. Therefore, his specific mention that "they don't want to be garbagemen" was very significant to me.

The comment about his cooking and his juicer also is very significant, because one of A.D.'s burdens in life, after my mother died, was cooking. He never really got into the swing of it. He finally got a juicer, which he enjoyed using, and made a very thorough study of nutrition and diet. He would often demonstrate the juicer to people who visited his cabin. (Margaret knew nothing about the juicer or his dislike of cooking.)

AN "ORIGINAL"

Later in the first sitting A.D. said, "Now, I don't want you to think of me as a typical minister. I don't want you to think of me as a typical anything, because I was an *original*."

This was said in jest, to make us laugh, but anyone who knew A.D. would agree that this was a good description of him. He was always many years ahead of his time in trying to lead the church out into the world to champion the causes of social justice and reform. His Commission on Morals and Social Problems of the Augustana Church, which he chaired for more than twenty-six years, was among the first Protestant church commissions to come forth with resolutions against racism and war and to deal with such problems as birth control and the population explosion.

When Karl Barth's theology, stressing that God is "wholly other," was at its peak, A.D. could not accept it. Instead, he went against the trend of the day and stressed the dynamic reality of the Kingdom of God. He recognized God as living and active, accomplishing His purposes in the realm of human history. A.D. saw this as a permanent dynamic for all time. He wrote:

> God is not geographically transcendent, in any faraway manner, on some celestial throne, waiting to be discovered by man. He is living and active and makes Himself known through His activity as He rules in His Kingdom. When this is recognized, theology becomes dynamic rather than static. It will then no longer be merely a matter of conserving and perpetuating doctrines, but it will concern itself with the resistance which is to be overcome and the great ends which are to be gained.[2]

DAHLIAS

When A.D. later described what my aura looks like to him during his communications, he said, "The rose pink comes out like big flower petals, like big spiky dahlia petals."

This did not strike me as evidential until I was transcribing the tapes, when I realized the significance of the specific mention of dahlia petals. Although A.D. appreciated most flowers, dahlias were his favorites, and at one time he grew many varieties of them with great success. When visiting us in New York, he enjoyed taking trips to the Bronx Botanical Gardens to view the dahlia beds.

ORANGE-COLORED CHAIRS

On several occasions during communications Margaret received "pictures" and remarked, "They are sitting on orange-colored chairs, comfortable-looking orange-colored chairs."

With so much material coming through, I also didn't register this evidential until I was replaying some of the tapes when the manuscript was almost complete. The orange-colored chairs are very evidential. If A.D. was going to have a chair in the astral world, it would certainly be orange, as that was one of his favorite colors. He asked me to make orange drapes for his cabin in Minnesota, and he furnished it with orange chairs, kitchen bar stools, table, lamps and dressers.

WHOLEHEARTED COMMITMENT TO GOD

"There are very few who will throw themselves into the sea of the Holy Spirit," A.D. said at an early sitting. "Some merely put their toe in and tentatively feel it. The years of putting toes in are past, and the time has come to throw yourself in."

This, again, is very typically A.D. Tentative, halfway measures on the part of people in their relation to God and His kingdom were always a source of pain to A.D. He constantly urged a wholehearted and courageous witness for God and His purposes in the world.

A.D.'S FATHER

In the first sitting, A.D. mentioned contacts with certain relatives who were dead, but did not mention his father. In the second sitting, I asked if he had seen his father.

A.D. said, "Strangely enough, yes, because I hadn't appreciated how important it would be to me. I had rather thought that I would need the help of my mother, of my wife, and maybe of my brother. But somehow or other, my father's impression on earth had formed me in a certain way, and I didn't feel that this certain way would need to be picked up anymore. But Father has been extremely helpful to me in adjusting to the conditions of this new life. He is a dear soul and has made a great deal of progress and really is way beyond me at the moment."

When they were both on earth, the views of A.D. and his father differed greatly and were sometimes a source of contention. A.D.'s father was a Lutheran minister with a rather pietistic approach to religion and life, and he had been a stern disciplinarian in enforcing his pietistic beliefs. But A.D. was nonpietistic, very undogmatic, and open in his outlook on life. Therefore, A.D.'s statement that he hadn't appreciated that he would need the help of his father when he passed over is evidential.

THE AMOS NOTES

A.D. mentioned that he had never finished a series of talks and lessons on the Bible that he had been giving. He said that I should surely have found some notes that he had ready for use, and that I had his full permission to use them any time I liked. They were there to be used.

I did find these notes in a zippered leather envelope at his cabin.

They were on the Book of Amos. He had been conducting a study on the Book of Amos for a group of people who lived near the Minnesota lake where his cabin was located.

"DON'T WEEP"

During the second sitting, when A.D. was describing the experience of his death to Margaret and me, I couldn't help crying. He said to me, "Don't cry, Ruth. You didn't cry then. What are you crying for now?"

This was very significant and evidential to me. My brother, Al, and I had been at A.D.'s bedside when he died. Al and I had stood on either side of his bed, holding his arms as he was going out. I had made up my mind that I would not cry, as I wanted him to be released without any sense of being held back by tears I might shed. (Margaret didn't know that I had not wept when I witnessed A.D.'s death.)

FAVORITE FLANNEL SHIRT

In the third session, Margaret was given a "picture" of A.D.'s reception by his family and friends when he passed over. After a description of some of the people who met him, Margaret said to me, "They seem to be wearing ordinary clothes—shirts, short-sleeved shirts, white knit shirts, trousers. They don't seem to be dressed in robes. Your father, as well, is dressed in gray trousers and he has a checked shirt on." A.D. had a checked flannel shirt that he always enjoyed wearing. "His favorite checked flannel shirt?" I asked, describing it. Margaret said it was.

Margaret then took time out to tell me that her sister, after she died, always appeared to clairvoyants in a favorite checked suit that she had enjoyed wearing when she was on earth.

At that point A.D. said to us, "That is perfectly right. You see, you have to think yourself into clothes over here. Your sister found it easier always to appear in her checked suit, which everyone recognized. So it was with me. When I was on earth, I didn't even think about clothes. I'd get up in the morning and I'd put on the first thing that was handy. Well, I stepped out of the physical body at the hospital and picked up the first clothes that were handy."

I didn't know what A.D. had worn to the hospital when he became ill. My brother had taken him to the hospital, and Al later told me that A.D. had worn gray trousers and his favorite checked flannel shirt. Al and I both felt that this was certainly good evidential.

INNER DYNAMO

In the second group of sittings, A.D. said, "When I was on earth, there was always with me a sense of urgency. I frequently felt, when I was going around among people, that there was a dynamo going inside of me that said, 'You haven't got much time. You must do this. You must do that.' I would sit back in my chair and try to relax, and I would look at people who seemed to be going along rather quietly, and I would wonder, 'Why should I have this feeling?'

"I had always imagined, as a younger man, that when I got toward 'old age' I would be quite content to sit back and browse in my thinking and watch the world go by. Somehow it didn't happen that way. In the days when I was a young man, I was chasing around the countryside or racing through books. Now in my 'old age' I was getting just as much activity going in my mind, in the narrow confines of where I was, as in the days when I traveled hundreds of miles. I realized that this pushing and driving was the accumulation of the things that needed to be done—pushing, pushing toward me. It made me feel as if there was this whirring dynamo inside me, which gave me energy."

Anyone who knew A.D. will testify to the dynamic movement in his life up to the very end. The sermon preached by the Reverend Allen C. Nelson at A.D.'s funeral illustrates this evidential:

"If only in this life..." says Paul. There was a tentativeness about life (says Paul), an uncertainty. This A.D. understood. There was something incomplete about life. But the now was significant. A.D. relished life. He savored its goodness. Each day spelled opportunity for him. He did not bask in the light of prior accomplishments but sought new avenues of service in his retirement years. "This is the day that the Lord has made. Let us rejoice and be glad in it." This he believed and lived. He did not settle into a comfortable niche. In his life there was movement. When you confronted A.D. and you sought to nail him down so you'd be quite sure that when you returned you'd find him there, you'd be doomed to disappointment. The now was not something simply to be accepted but to be acted upon.[3]

CONSTANT JOHNSON

On February 28, 1972, we had a very objective evidential incident. Before a sitting on that day Margaret said to me, "Who is Constant Johnson? Your father tells me that he has not been well and that he will soon be over with them." The Reverend Dr. Constant Johnson and A.D. were classmates in their seminary days, and he was a well-known clergyman in the Augustana Lutheran Church. I had known him when I was a little girl but certainly had not thought about him in many years, nor had I had any contact with him or his family. I certainly knew nothing about his health, or even if he were alive or dead. I decided to watch the obituary notices in *The Lutheran*, and, sure enough, in the April 19, 1972, issue of this magazine I found a notice of Dr. Constant Johnson's death, which occurred on March 14, 1972.[4]

MARGARET,
THE CLAIRVOYANT

One may see the Way of Heaven without looking through the windows.

LAO TZU

MANY PEOPLE WHO read *Witness from Beyond* have asked me how I came to know Margaret, and I always tell them that I believe that I was led by the spirit of God to make the connection with her.

My brother, Al, the Reverend A.D. Mattson, Jr., was pastor of the Lutheran church in Anaconda, Montana. Like the rest of our family, he had been particularly interested in paranormal phenomena. In Anaconda he met Mona Beal, wife of a prominent dentist and a woman with unusual mystic gifts. He had been unable to share his enthusiastic interest in the paranormal with people in his congregation, but he found Mona Beal to be a kindred spirit in this area. He learned much from her and valued her friendship.

Al later moved to Missoula, Montana, to become Lutheran campus pastor at the University of Montana, and from there he later moved with his family to Hartford, Connecticut, to study for his Ph.D. at Hartford Seminary.

While Al was in Connecticut, he and his family would often drive in on weekends to visit us at our home in Scarsdale, New York. One weekend when they were with us, Al told me that his friend Mona Beal was visiting her daughter, Donna Piana, in Rye, New York, a suburb near our home, and that he would very much like to have me meet her. Though Donna had a previous engagement, we arranged to meet Mona at her home that afternoon. We had a wonderful visit together, and I found Mona to be a very "inspired" person.

A short while after that visit, and after Mona had returned to Montana, her daughter, Donna, phoned to invite me to join the group that met at her home every Thursday morning for prayer and meditation. She said that Mona felt very strongly that I should be in that group. I was very busy at the time with my work for religious journals, and I declined the invitation with thanks.

Donna continued to call me, and I finally decided to accept her invitation to see if I really wanted to participate in the group. I went over to her home, and I found the meeting to be one of the most inspirational that I had ever attended. The group was comprised of eight women of different religious persuasions, all devoted to spiritual development and values. From then on, I never missed a Thursday morning at Donna's home if I could possibly help it. My own spiritual opening and development there was more than I could have hoped for.

Jane Evans, a member of the group, had lived in England and was a very close friend of Margaret Flavell. On a visit to the United States, Margaret came to Rye to visit Jane, and Jane brought her to our Thursday-morning session, where we met. The threads of spiritual weaving from my brother's friendship with Mona Beal in Anaconda to bringing Margaret and me together in Rye, New York, had completed their pattern. That meeting resulted in a thirty-year friendship and close association in the realm of inter-life communication.

To experience a sitting with Margaret Flavell is to become convinced of the marvelous gifts with which she is endowed and of her integrity and dedication. The Reverend Canon Berton S. Levering, Rector Emeritus of All Saints Episcopal Church in Detroit, a man of outstanding repute who had known Margaret for many years, said of her:

> "Margaret Flavell is a brilliant translator of thought communication from the world of the departed. Her early training in the London School of Paranormal Psychology and Sanctuary of Healing established a foundation of expanded spiritual awareness that has continued to grow. One feels her integrity of mind and deep sense of responsibility as she makes known the continuity of life. Her common sense, humility of spirit and dedication, illuminated by a fine sense of humor, enable her to share her experience with others."[5]

When I met Margaret, I knew of course that she was a clairvoyant. My mother had died in November 1960, and on many occasions I had felt that she was very close to me, and that she wanted to get through to me. I had an opportunity to talk to Margaret about this when we were left alone in Donna's living room while the other members of the group were out in the kitchen preparing a snack. I really had no idea of how such things were accomplished, and I thought that perhaps Margaret would suggest that we set up a séance to see if we could get through to my mother.

It was ten o'clock in the morning on a bright, sunny day, and all of a sudden, right there in Donna's lovely, cheerful living room, Margaret said to me: "Your mother is here now, and there are three other persons with her."

The others proved to be my deceased uncle, Karl Mattson, who had been president of the Augustana Seminary in Rock Island, Illinois; my husband's uncle, Dr. Wilbur Bowen, who had been my own physician and had died as a result of a car accident; and my maternal grandmother, Johanna Anderson. The evidential material that came through on all of them was overwhelming and indisputable. I could have fallen right off my chair. Margaret had never met me or any other member of my family before. It was a meaningful and uplifting experience, and one that I have never forgotten.

Some of the evidence from my mother, surprisingly, dealt with china dishes. (And I had always thought that contact with the Beyond would be of a very profound nature!) Through that sitting I learned that our personalities do not change much when we die. My mother had always treasured her collection of fine china, which was still at my father's home in Rock Island, Illinois. She expressed great concern that the dishes might be broken, and she told Margaret that I should have certain specific pieces shipped to my home in New York. Also, she told us of a beautiful cut-glass vase (of which I knew nothing) in a cupboard in the house in Rock Island. She wanted this vase to be made into a lamp for my brother and his wife. My father and I located the vase in the cupboard, exactly where Mother said it would be, and we had it made into a beautiful lamp for Al and his wife, Jean. (More than ten years later, in our first sitting with A.D. after his death, he told Margaret that he found it easy to communicate with her on the "thread" of communication that had been made first by my mother on that lovely day in Rye, New York.)

Over the years I have come to know Margaret not only as a gifted clairvoyant but also as a close friend. A Methodist by background, she is a deeply religious person. She has been a frequent leader at spiritual retreats both in the United Kingdom and the United States, using her special abilities to help others deepen their faith and to become more God-centered. Since World War II, she has ministered in Spiritualist churches throughout England.

Among the psychical research community in England, Margaret is well known and respected for her accomplishments in that field. A born clairvoyant, she was highly trained over many years in the control of her natural psychic gifts through daily controlled experiments and disciplines. A graduate of the London School of Paranormal Psychology and Sanctuary of Healing, she later was assistant to Dr. Mona Rolfe, founder and director of the school.

Margaret is one of the rare positive mediums who receive while in full control and not in trance. During World War II, at the request of Lord Hugh Dowding, Marshal of the Royal Air Force, she and Dr. Rolfe collaborated in psychometry (clairvoyance in which an object belonging to a person is used to aid the process) to trace many missing fliers, both alive and deceased, with a high degree of accuracy.

A very down-to-earth person, Margaret has been a teacher of English and foreign languages. This experience helped to create a vast vocabulary that is extremely useful in receiving communications. In addition to being a lecturer and spiritual counselor and healer, she has also worked in publishing, printing, and market research.

Margaret and A.D. never met while he was on earth, which has made the evidential material of A.D.'s communications, as well as the nuances of his personality that come through, all the more significant. Margaret is a highly intelligent woman with a good sense of humor, which has made her an ideal match for A.D. in communicating with good rapport.

RUTH,
YOUR GUIDE

The grand difficulty is to feel the reality of both worlds, so as to give each its due place in our thoughts and feelings: to keep our mind's eye and our heart's eye ever fixed on the land of promise, without looking away from the road along which we are to travel toward it.

AUGUST W. AND JULIUS C. HARE

BEING THE DAUGHTER of A.D. and Freda Mattson has been a blessing and a rich experience in many ways. They were parents who provided strong family bonds for my brother, Al, and me. They nurtured us in the Christian faith, yet taught us to respect and learn from other religions and cultures too. A.D. always told us, "Truth is Truth, wherever it is found." We attended services of many religions for a sense of brotherhood with all mankind.

Our parents also gave us opportunities to know people of all races. I recall, when I was a very little girl, the visits of Alaskan Eskimo Chief Harry Soxie to our home in Minnesota. When we lived in Rock Island, Illinois, there were regular Sunday suppers in our home with both black and white seminary students at our table. In the summers when A.D.

was serving congregations in the Dakotas, he enthusiastically took us to the Native American celebrations and sun dances. As a child, I also had the privilege of meeting Kagawa, the great Japanese Christian. All of these experiences enriched my life, and I have been grateful to feel a strong bond with all people.

Being present when A.D. was struggling for social justice over the years also made a very deep impression on me.

Most of my life was lived in Rock Island, where A.D. taught in our Lutheran seminary. While in Rock Island, I attended Augustana College and earned my A.B. degree in psychology with a strong minor in chemistry. My chemistry studies resulted in my training as a spectro-chemist at the Rock Island Arsenal metallurgical laboratory during my senior year of college. I was later employed by the Caterpillar Tractor Company in Peoria, Illinois, to set up their spectro-chemical laboratory during the early days of World War II.

After the war, I left Caterpillar to work on my master's degree in industrial psychology, first at the University of Wisconsin in Madison, and later at Northwestern University in Evanston, Illinois, where I completed the work for my Master of Science degree. My background and training in scientific research at the university have helped me to keep my perspective and be objective when dealing with our paranormal data on inter-life communication.

In 1948 I married Harold V. Taylor, and we lived for eight years in the Chicago area, where Hal was a network radio and TV producer for ABC. It was during those years that our son, Bruce, and daughter, Lynne, were born. Later we moved to New York, where Hal produced radio and TV commercials for twenty-four years. During that time, I established an advertising management business to serve religious journals. This work I continue to do, along with my exploration of inter-life communication.

My professional life in the area of inter-life communication includes an academic membership in the Academy of Religion and

Psychical Research, and memberships in Spiritual Frontiers Fellowship, the Spiritual Advisory Council, the Institute of Noetic Sciences, and the Association of Research and Enlightenment.

MY BROTHER, AL
(ALVIN DANIEL MATTSON, JR.)

Following in A.D.'s footsteps, my brother, Al, was ordained into the Lutheran ministry in 1952. He served as a parish pastor in Anaconda, Montana, and later became the Lutheran campus pastor at the University of Montana in Missoula. He and his wife, Jean, and their three children later moved to Hartford, Connecticut, where Al was enrolled in the doctoral program at Hartford Seminary. After Al completed his course work at that seminary, the family moved to Grand Forks, where he taught in the Department of Philosophy and Religion at the University of North Dakota. Only a short while later, Al died unexpectedly of a ruptured aneurysm, at the age of forty-five, just one day after receiving his Ph.D. from Hartford Seminary.

Al had been very interested in inter-life communication and, while at the University of North Dakota, he conducted experiments with an engineering student from India who was a trance medium. With Al's interest in these areas, it was natural that he, too, would communicate with us from the world beyond. When he communicates with us, I can easily distinguish the nuances of his personality from those of A.D. and other communicators. Al tells us of his continued interest in inter-life communication, and he's now studying these phenomena from the perspective of those in the realm beyond.

LED TO OUR HOUSE IN MAINE

The story of our house is perhaps one of the most evidential accounts I can share with you. After we moved to New York, Hal and I vacationed in Maine for many years, and we loved Maine more than any other place we had ever been. We agreed that we would like to live there permanently when Hal retired. We both loved the ocean, and our dream was to find a property on the water. We decided to look for a house in the Portland area.

In the summer of 1971, ten months after A.D.'s death, we began our search. In our very first attempt we found a lovely home that sat back from the water along the shipping channel. Although there was another house right on the water in front of it, the house we found was perfect for us, and it still had a good view of the bay. However, although we loved the house and the location, we still had it in the back of our minds that we really wanted to be directly on the water. We told the realtor that we would think about it, and that we would call him from New York in a few days.

After days of agonizing over whether it was the right place, we decided it was. We called the realtor, and, to our dismay, we found out that someone else had purchased the property just three hours before.

I was devastated! I agonized over the loss of that house a lot.

Margaret came to visit us a short time after that. We were having a sitting with A.D., and in that sitting, Margaret stopped and said, "A.D. tells me that you are going to have to stop agonizing over that house you lost, or they are not going to be able to replace it with the one you are meant to have. The house you are going to have is not far from the one you found, and you are going to like it a lot more than the first one."

Right after that sitting, Margaret and I went out to the dining room to have some lunch. When we were at the table, she suddenly looked up, stared ahead of her, and said, "Your house is going to have windows here and here"—she gestured, showing me where they would be—"across the back of the house, and these windows will face the sea, and there will be no houses between you and the sea, only brush." She also described other details, including a garden by a big rosebush at the back.

Margaret gave us that description of "our house" in 1971. Each year after that we kept looking and looking. Our realtor would bring us up winter and summer to view various properties, and none was right. Margaret began to wonder about her accuracy, and she said to her husband, "I was really wrong about this! Why don't they find that house?"

In April 1979 our son, Bruce, was receiving his doctorate from the University of Michigan, and we decided to go to Ann Arbor for the graduation ceremonies. We stayed at a motel near the airport. At the same time, Margaret was visiting her cousin Jessie in Southfield, a suburb near where we were staying. We were both very busy, and didn't manage to get together. However, we did speak on the phone, and in that phone conversation, Margaret said, "Ruth, I think you're about to find that house, and it's going to have a beamed-ceiling living room." That was on April 26th.

When we returned to New York, our niece Audrey was coming through the city on her way back to Seattle after studying in India for a year. She planned to stay a week with us. It was the end of May, and Memorial Day weekend. We asked Audrey if she would enjoy a trip to Maine for a few days, and she said she would. We arranged to stay in Kennebunkport, and took Audrey and our daughter, Lynne, along on the trip. On Friday of that weekend Hal and I decided to go up to Portland once again to look for the house. The two girls remained in Kennebunkport to windowshop and enjoy some time on the beach.

Eight years had now passed since Margaret first described our future house to us. The realtor who patiently searched for many years had moved to Nevada. Another member of that real estate office took us around that day. When we couldn't find what we wanted, he suggested that he take us over to a neighborhood on the shipping channel in South Portland, because his sister had her house on the market in that neighborhood. He said it wasn't on the water, but that it was a very nice house and an exceptional neighborhood.

The house *was* lovely, but we really had our hearts set on a waterfront location. As he drove us away, he followed the street down a steep hill. At the bottom of the hill, he turned at the water—and there stood our house, exactly as Margaret had described it!

I quickly told the realtor that if that house were ever for sale, *that* was what we were looking for. The realtor told us that he knew the woman who owned the house, and that he had been meaning to ask her if she was interested in selling. She was a widow, had been living there for eighteen years, and it was a large house for one person. He said she was in Europe on vacation, but that he would talk with her when she returned.

Hal and I returned to New York, and three weeks later the phone rang. It was our realtor. He said that the woman who owned the house we wanted had returned from Europe and that she did intend to sell her house. She had just bought a condominium in Falmouth. She was willing to show her house to us before she put it on the market. He told us to come up right away, which we did.

When we walked into the house for the first time, we fell in love with it. We found the most beautiful beamed-ceiling living room, just as Margaret had said! The other details were also just as Margaret had described them to us. We were ecstatic! The location was right on the water, where we could watch the ever-changing sea. This wonderful house was much more suitable for us than the first house would have been, just as A.D. had said it would be.

All in God's good time His gifts are given to us.

HAL JOINS A.D. AND AL

We moved to our house in June 1980. Hal lived eight and one half more years to enjoy our wonderful home by the sea. He'd had open-heart surgery twelve years before in New York, and he died of congestive heart failure on January 11, 1989. I have missed his physical presence greatly, but I still feel his love and support through his spiritual presence. He, too, communicates with us from the world beyond, and also has made his presence known through a number of telekinetic manifestations. They are presented in Part Four, at the end of this book. That section also includes a special message from him about his own experiences in the world beyond.

PART TWO

THE ROAD

HOW THE TWO WORLDS
COMMUNICATE

*There is a limit where the intellect fails and breaks down, and
this limit is where the questions concerning God, and
freewill, and immortality arise.*

KANT

I THINK THERE ARE several reasons why, of the many theologians who
have died, A.D. is able to communicate hundreds of pages of material
while others have gotten only scraps of information through.

First of all, A.D. had a great desire to come back and share experiences with us. On numerous occasions he told us that when he died he
was surely going to try to communicate back to earth. In many of the
sittings we've been aware that it requires a lot of discipline and training for him to do this.

Second, A.D. and I were very close when he was on earth. We were
both deeply interested in psychic research, and we often had long dis-
cussions about developments in that field. Margaret and I also share a
close friendship and respect. These ties, I'm sure, are a big factor in the
ease of communication we experience.

Third, A.D. may be given the privilege of communicating exten-
sively because, although he was highly educated in theology, he was

always able to relate well to all people. This is one of the virtues of communications received from him: They are simple and clear, and they come through to Margaret in the same warm, friendly manner he was loved for on earth.

Though another close friend was present a couple of times, usually only Margaret and I were in the room during a communication session. We would set aside a specific time to have a sitting, then send a thought to A.D. to let him know when we would be ready. At the appointed hour, we would sit quietly in the room and begin with silent meditation. When A.D. arrived and was ready to communicate, he often would begin with a prayer, such as, "Let the words of my mouth and the meditations of our hearts be acceptable in Thy sight, O Lord, our strength and our Redeemer."

Once the communication began, I, as the listener, would continue to sit silently and monitor the taping process. As I mentioned earlier, Margaret is a "positive" medium and doesn't need to go into trance. It is as though she were relaying a phone conversation, and it is her voice that is recorded on the tape although changes in character can be perceived when different communicators come through. The earliest sessions lasted only about a half hour, because A.D. wasn't able to "hold" the line of communication any longer. Now that he's more accustomed to communicating, sessions run as long as forty-five minutes to an hour.

VISIBLE AURAS

In our very first sitting, when contact was made, A.D. said, "Margaret, I see you as a combination of many colors, and I know I am communicating to you. I see you as a gray shape with flashing colors around you. When you two were in silent meditation at the beginning of the sitting, the colors of both your auras began to come down into regular bands. When they became a little still and only vibrated a little, that was the signal for us to begin to communicate. I was told to wait. If I rush in prematurely, I get a word or two through, but then there isn't a continuous, harmonious communication.

"With Ruth, I can see much green and blue, a great deal of blue and a mass of rose pink. The rose pink comes out like big flower petals— like big spiky dahlia petals—like funnels. That's your affection and your love going out. This you mustn't spread too far and wide, too frequently, without asking for the Lord to replenish you."

Later, when listening to our first tape, a parapsychologist wondered about A.D.'s comment on seeing Margaret as a gray shape. Margaret and I talked about this in January 1972 before a sitting. A.D. overheard our conversation, and in the sitting that followed, he said, "You made me smile, because many people see us as gray shapes, ghosts, apparitions. Why should he feel surprised that we might see you in the same way that you see us?"

Nevertheless, there seems to be a gradual development of astral sight, because on October 6, 1972, A.D. said to us, "Now, my children, I want you to know that I'm beginning to see the bodies of people on earth very clearly."

LIGHT OF BODY

On another occasion A.D. said, "Margaret, you know what it is like to be light of body because the minute we begin to communicate, you lose your sense of heaviness of body."

Margaret's face lit up and she said to me, "You know, that's absolutely true, Ruth, and I've never had anybody else describe it to me. I do feel that way when I've got a good communication. I'm not aware of how heavy my legs are, and if I move my legs, they feel as if they are going to float off somewhere and my feet will go off from the end of them."

A.D. then continued, "You, Ruth, could take this as a measure for yourself. When you have lost the feeling of the weight of your body, then you know that you are getting your inner self."

BACKGROUND MUSIC

After my brother, Al, died, he occasionally joined A.D. at our sessions. It was Al who told us of the importance of music in paving the way for messages to reach their destination:

"Soft music as a background when we're communicating with you makes for easier communication," he said. "The music forms patterns that break down coarser patterns in your atmosphere that prevent the best communication between us. There is far better intercommunication with soft music as a background."

CONVEYING MESSAGES

Transporting thoughts between our worlds is a complicated process. A.D. has given us detailed explanations, and in a session with Margaret and me in 1993, he pointed out that the method changes subtly on the different planes of existence in the world beyond:

"This process of communication is a difficult one to explain. My thought pattern changes on the various planes of existence. It is more nebulous on the mental level where I now function, and I find it more difficult to come in and be grounded. Coming here to you both now, I receive much energy and power and solidity in grounding. I need to reaffirm this sense of 'base' every now and then. I plan to be around you, Ruth, when you are writing, since that will not only assist you, but will help me again feel more firmly in touch with earth matters. There is so much upheaval on earth now, and I feel a need and pressure to try to help. That's why I need to plant my feet more firmly, once again."

In *Witness from Beyond*, A.D. and Margaret explained more fully how their communication works. For the benefit of new friends, and to refresh the memory of old friends, their messages on how they bridge the distance between our two worlds are repeated here.

A MESSAGE FROM A.D.

Man can learn nothing unless he proceeds from the known to the unknown.

CLAUDE BERNARD

I HAVEN'T YET BECOME accustomed to all the words, the jargon, concerning communication, so I am trying to keep it simple. A good receiver is one who, as though winding a skein of wool, keeps one end and winds it up carefully, carefully, like that tape is winding—listening and not allowing any thought to come in except what is actually being given to her by the communicator. The early mediums did not have the necessary control of their brain and their mind to clear away all thought and allow the communication to come through. That is why there had to be trance mediumship.

THOUGHT PROJECTION

One of the real reasons for a great deal of frustration is the fact that I can only send a thought to Margaret, and she must translate that thought into words. As you are aware, I have stopped her on more than one occasion so that she will pick up the right word to interpret what my thought and meaning is. I am projecting my thought to Margaret without using words because it is slow and laborious for me to use words.

It is vitally important for you to realize that, when you get a message, you should not condemn it and say, "But that's not his speech. That's not the way he talks." I am not talking words. I am sending a thought from my mind to Margaret's mind, and her personality and brain have to interpret it.

THE STREAM OF LIFE—THE HOLY SPIRIT

We have to tell all people who mourn that they must be comforted because unless they are comforted, we can't get through to them.

There is this stream of life, the Holy Spirit, and it is like a spring coming up. It comes up into the pool of your own consciousness. If your own consciousness is so turbulent, the spring as it comes from the ground is taken up with all this turbulence.

If you take a still pool and you place a spring at the back of it, water would come from the spring and it would move through the pool so that all you would see would be currents moving through the water until they come to the surface.

When we communicate, this is how you should feel—that the Holy Spirit is like that spring in you and you receive through the calmness of your own consciousness.

If you can't understand it any other way, fill up a bathtub with water, and then put a tube on a faucet and put the tube at the bottom. Now let the water into the bath, and you'll see how it makes patterns as it comes up, patterns as it infiltrates in the stillness of the bathwater. This is exactly how the picture seems to me as I look at you, Margaret. You have this stillness, and through the spring of the Holy Spirit I am communicating with you. This movement is made spirit to spirit, and these movements impinge on the brain and the brain coats them in words.

It is true that I have my material prepared. I also find that I am inclined to link in a little with your minds. When you seem to be more interested in one thing, then I enlarge on that, extending the area of information, and widening the scope of the subject. I can also at times pick up from your minds the questions you want to ask me, and I can also pick up your questions when you write them out on paper.

THE CIRCULAR MUSHROOM

When I communicate with you, I have my own little area—a little round circular mushroomlike place. It really *is* a very large white mushroom. It has quilting material underneath, which is for the acoustics, and I do sit there and broadcast my thoughts to you. I can pick up through that crinkle, crinkle, crinkle material of the ceiling. I pick up your responses to me very carefully. They come, and I pick them up at the back of my neck. There are those with me who are working on this. It's rather like a recording studio. They know when I'm in full bore, and they turn down the power a bit. They know when I'm wavering a bit, and when I'm slowly feeling my way in. It's a new experience to be able to see what people think by the light and thought and colors and emanations that come up from them.

An interesting point has just arisen. I was finding myself so easily projecting to you and receiving your link in reply in a much clearer way than usual. I remarked on this, and was told that it is raining hard, and we find the humid atmosphere conducive to good reception on this side.[6]

A MESSAGE
FROM MARGARET

All I have seen teaches me to trust the Creator for all I have not seen.

EMERSON

IT IS VERY DIFFICULT to translate into words what a medium experiences during communication, but I'll try to convey it as well as I can.

I relax completely, quiet the mind and brain, hold in "stillness," and disassociate from the physical. In the stillness, I become aware of a different vibration that is insistent and continuous in its feel.

On questing, I become aware of receiving a thought that is foreign. This thought develops and I become aware of a projected personality. On inquiring, a name/personality develops and, as over a telephone, a reciprocal conversation takes place.

At times a picture of the person comes, as well as the personality traits. For example, I have seen A.D. in various places: under a canopy, which he described; sitting on a chair in various locations, which we also discussed. The first time of meeting I saw him in his favorite checked shirt and flannel trousers.

A continuous conversation, mind to mind, deepens until A.D., smoothly as in a physical conversation, expresses thoughts and feelings.

Sometimes the feelings received have caused laughter or tears. The latter I can register and feel with him. This may be called empathy.

The whole contact is on a mind-to-mind basis—no trance—for I never leave my body. I am aware of where I am—in a room or in a car. A.D. communicated some information to me in my car, in a parking lot at the hospital, and this information I wrote down on paper rather than recording it on tape. It is possible to accept the thought without being aware of the presence of the communicator as a person, but A.D. generally projects his whole personality while sending his thoughts, so that anyone hearing his recorded talk recognizes him. The effect is quite different from the reply one receives in asking a question of the ether, not sending it to any particular personality or mind. Then the reply is in a flash. One may wait for quite a period of time for a communicator to come through.

In 1971 I awoke one morning aware of a message A.D. had given me during the night. He said he didn't wake me up. I was already in the process of waking. He had left the message for me to pick up. It gives me the idea that they must have some kind of an answering service—they put it on a cassette and we switch it on when we wake. [Margaret laughed a bit about this, and then continued:] A.D. says I'm not to laugh, because there's more to that than he knows. He can't explain it at the present time, because he doesn't really know how it works. However, he can project a thought to me, and it doesn't register until later when my brain begins to interpret what my mind has received. He told me that our mind is like a desk with a lot of pigeonholes. They can put information in, and when our brain is moving along, the mind slips the information in, as it slipped it in this morning, just as I was waking.

A VORTEX OF POWER

In Ruth's home, A.D. enters a vortex of power, which is like a movement of power, like a cone of power. He can come into that power and everything else is cut out for the time being. He is just himself in what looks to me like a spiral of power. It is going continuously—coming down and going up again—rather like an old-fashioned barber pole of light and power. It's about four feet across the top as I see it, and it narrows down like a funnel. A.D. is projecting his thinking down through that. It's very easy to do it here, because this atmosphere is steady and holds the communication. He says that is one reason why he said to us on the way home this morning that we should not go into the middle of a restaurant to eat lunch, because that confusion remains in my aura, and then he can't get through very easily.[7]

PART THREE

THE JOURNEY BEGINS

AS WE START ON OUR WAY

"Rise ye up, take your journey..."
DEUTERONOMY 2:24

THE BEAUTIFUL JOURNEY we are about to take is a continuation of the one we set off on in 1971 when A.D. first began to communicate with us. His messages and discoveries from that year through 1973 are shared in *Witness from Beyond*. The messages that follow were received after that time, many in sittings in 1993 and most recently in May 1996.

There is much information A.D. wants to share with us, about the world beyond and about our own world too. I have divided it according to subject, and at the beginning of each chapter, I provide explanations and background information that may be helpful to the reader. That information is followed by this ornament: ——. The chapter itself, just as the introduction that follows below, is always in A.D.'s own words.

———

WHAT I WANT to emphasize is that what I gave you when we sat before were my impressions as *me*, A.D., newly arrived after my death. I now want to give you, if I can, some of the thoughts that come to me, clothed with my new thinking, because I do think differently now. I think I am in the process of change. However, this changing is not cutting me off from the world, or making me feel separate from the world and the people I left behind. It is making me feel closer, more knit, as if the web of my being is intermingled and weaving in with the beings of all of you. I have a feeling of a closer affinity with all people, and with all thoughts and ideas.

I have been expanding in my consciousness, and have been expanding in my understanding of laws that maybe I had read about but had not utilized or understood. Life, both here and on earth, is always expanding. In these communications I want to speak in a practical, everyday manner that will be meaningful to the average person. In my personal, everyday life on earth I thought and spoke in a down-to-earth, practical manner. I didn't talk about theology to the fisherman who came and sat and fished off my property at the lake. I spoke with the fisherman about fish and flies, and water, and God immanent and God transcendent in nature. So here, too, I want to speak about things that will be meaningful to the average person.

Also, I want to stress that this is *my* impression—I give it as I see it. Others may see it differently. Those who are wiser than I am have written about the universe in many different ways. I intend to convey to you only what I see, and my own impressions of what I understand at my present state of development.

AS SUN IS TO MOON,
SO LIFE IS TO DEATH

When the perishable has been clothed with the imperishable, and the mortal with immortality, then the saying that is written will come true: "Death has been swallowed up in victory."

1 CORINTHIANS 15:54

THROUGHOUT HIS LIFE, A.D. taught us that there is no need to fear death, and now, in an allegory comparing life and death to the sun and moon, he brings that message from the world beyond. He also tells us that it is not good, either for ourselves or for our loved ones who have died, to hold on to unhealthy grief. Although we deeply miss our loved ones who have made their transition to the realm beyond, A.D. tells us that we should try to have a sense of closeness and celebration with them, knowing that, although they have gone on to a far more glorious realm, they still continue to support us with their presence and love.

THE SUN IS a source of power from God that reflects onto the moon. When the sun is up above the earth's horizon, we are unable to experience the full benefit of its reflection on the moon. During those hours, the light of the moon is submerged in the daylight. However, when the sun goes down below the horizon at night, then the moon is clearly and brilliantly reflected in the dark sky.

I want to use this as an allegory to tell people that they do not need to fear death. There is a spiritual self within, which, like the moon in the daytime sky, is not very prominent. This is because we move around in the physical body, which, like the daylight, submerges the spiritual self. But the Spiritual Light of God, like the sun, is always present. When night comes and we go into the dark that we call death, then the reflection of the Spiritual Light of God is far stronger on us. Then we are fully aware of our spiritual selves.

We may think that when we die we're going into the dark, but the Spiritual Light of God shines through death and illuminates our spiritual self all the more strongly. As the moon appears so much brighter in the sky at night, when the sun has disappeared from the horizon, so the Life Force of God reflects through the bodies that we live in when we go into the dark that we call death. The Light and Power of God illuminates and sustains the inner you that goes on, so why be afraid of death?

It seems to me that the very early peoples of the earth were much nearer the great Truth that life is everlasting than many people are today. For instance, they believed that life went on, and so they placed the favorite beaker, or arrow, or bead necklace of loved ones in their graves, because they were sure that those objects would still be needed in the afterlife. In today's services, where they hear "ashes to ashes" and "dust to dust," onlookers often believe that the whole person has indeed gone into that grave. Rather, we should stress that only the physical body has gone into the grave or has been cremated, and that the inner self is more alive than before.

Like Jesus on Easter Sunday, the shining inner self is risen. It is alive, and it is going around and it is cognizant of what it is doing. It's hard for me to appreciate now what it must be like to be afraid to die.

When you're dead, you very quickly become accustomed to it, and you feel that you are very much alive.

DO NOT GRIEVE FOR US

Churches have taught people how to live, but they have not taught people how to die. Nor have they made it clear that unhealthy grief is no good for either the living or the dead. It is important for you on earth to realize that you must not cling to unhealthy grief for us. You should strive to adjust to the separation, and to recognize that your loved one has gone on and is living a fulfilling life, even though separated from you. If you on earth continue to grieve and allow that grief to impinge on your life in such a way that you are continually sad and not functioning to your best capacity and development, that draws us back to see you in your grief. This causes us much concern. That concern—our grief for you in your unhappiness—hinders our own growth and development. For when we grieve for you, we cannot feel the freedom and joy intended for us here.

Often on the anniversary of the death of a loved one, people on earth spend the day literally agonizing in their grief. This is very counterproductive for the souls who have died. These souls are busy getting constructive lives established, and they are suddenly pulled back to those loved ones who are steeped in grief. This is very disruptive and upsetting to the one who is on the spiritual planes.

We want you to use the anniversary of our death as a remembrance of our life with you. We want you to have a sense of closeness and celebration with us on that day. You should concentrate on the fact that we have gone on to an even more wonderful life. We want you to know that, though unseen, we still continue to support you with our "presence" and love.

FAITH IN THE PRESENCE
OF THE UNSEEN

...[W]e are always confident and know that as long as we are at home in the body we are away from the Lord. We live by faith, not by sight.

2 CORINTHIANS 5:6–7

FAITH WAS ALWAYS important to A.D. Here he speaks about our need to use faith when dealing with the unseen. In the presence of the unseen, we are faced with the intangible. We are dealing with the mind, and no one can touch the mind. It is impossible to put a finger on a cell in the physical body and say, "This is the mind," as we can do with the brain and other physical organs of the body. He reveals that it also took a great deal of faith for him in the realm beyond to realize that he could indeed communicate with us here. Faith, he tells us, is the basis of all creativity. It is even an act of faith to live.

———◆———

I WANT TO PAUSE a bit with you and think about faith. When you begin to deal with things unseen and intangible to the physical self, you need faith.

Scientists will test a theory until they have something tangible, and then that is their proof. They then must see how many times there is a repetition that proves their theory is correct and true. But in dealing with the unseen, which can't be tested by our five senses, faith must be relied on.

No one can touch the mind. It is impossible to put a finger on a cell in the physical body and say, "This is the mind." We may put a finger on cells in the body and say, "This is a kidney, this is the heart, this is the throat, and this is the brain." But when you say *the mind*, when you say *the soul*, then you are using faith. You believe that there is this mind, because it motivates the whole physical body, and it motivates other people.

A great proportion of a spiritual leader's time is spent in using his own faith in the things unseen. Yet, when people come for help or counseling, how can he share that faith with them? He can't just bestow it on them as he could bestow a pound of sugar, or a rose from his garden, or even a text out of the Bible. He has to give it to them by his mode, by his method, his way of speaking, his way of living, his way of ordering his life.

This is where the difficulty comes. Those of you who have faith, how do you demonstrate it? There can be no absolute certainty that you have demonstrated it until it is received. It is like offering a gift. You may send a gift through the mail. You've wrapped it, you've addressed it, and you've taken it to the post office. It's stamped and it's gone. But not until you receive a reply from the recipient do you know that your gift has been received.

It's the same way when you hand faith to someone. You demonstrate faith to that person. You offer it to him as a gift—a gift of God. But it isn't until you see faith working in him that you can know he has truly received this gift of God.

We also have to remember that not everyone uses the spiritual gifts in the same way. And that is very fortunate. How boring it would be if we all expressed our faith in the same way! Fortunately for each one of us, there is always the element of surprise: "Oh, so *that* is the way he sees it, and *that* is the way he uses that gift, force, or attribute," we say. "Now, I don't use it that way. I use it *this* way." It is wrong for any of us, incarnate or discarnate, to say to anyone, "You should do it this way, because I do it this way." Each person is unique and will express God's gifts according to his or her own faith and understanding.

It took a great deal of faith for me to believe that I could send a thought down to that shape sitting there on that chair [Margaret], and to be confident that my thought would arrive resembling what I sent. That took faith. So, please, let people know that in coming back to communicate, we, too, must have faith.

Sometimes I meet people here who say, "You know, I try to make a link with my wife, and it's no good at all. I just can't get through, and I feel so disappointed." And I ask, "Did your wife expect that link?" The answer is often something like, "Well, she's a good Christian and goes to church."

My advice then is for him to see if he can get through to his minister, who in turn can give the thought to the man's wife that, "Maybe Jack is trying to get through to you. He hasn't just gone off, never to be near you again."

The moment that there is even a little chink in the door like that, then Jack can go and put the warmth of love around his wife, and he can begin to say, "I'm here." Maybe he will *never* get through, but maybe he will. All I'm saying is that you can't do anything without faith.

I don't know if I've made myself clear. There is so much bound up in faith that sometimes I feel I will burst. I used to feel like that even when I was in the physical body on earth, because, to me, the Love of God is the basis of all things, and that Love has to *demonstrate* itself through us. Faith is the foundation of that demonstration.

Please remember that living itself is an act of faith. You can't do anything without faith. Look on yourselves as mirrors to reflect the

Light of God, which is given to you through your faith. The Light is passed to you, and that Light must not be hidden under a bushel.

In the presence of death, have faith that life is like a train. Even though at the end of life it may seem as if you are in a dark tunnel, know that the tracks are still under you. The engine or energy is still pulling you toward the end of the tunnel—into the Realm of Light.

THE PLANES OF EXISTENCE

It is a profound mistake to think that everything has been discovered; as well think the horizon to be the boundary of the world.

Antoine Marin Lemierre

Much has been written about the concept of different planes of existence or levels of consciousness. Even the Bible refers to the *heavens* in the plural and, in 2 Corinthians 12:2, Saint Paul refers to being caught up to the *third heaven*. A.D. has discovered this is true, and he shares with us what he has learned about these planes, or heavens. The world beyond is not "up there" somewhere—its various planes are simply different conditions of the same space. The planes have different densities or vibrations, though, which is why, unless we are clairvoyant, we can't see people who have died.

The astral plane where we go immediately after death is almost a replica of our world, except that it is of a finer substance. This gives a sense of continuity, and it enables the souls who have died to make an easier transition to their new state of being. It was sweet and comforting to learn that animals survive in the realm beyond too. Our beloved pets are lovingly cared for there until we rejoin them.

When people who have been ill die, they still carry over that illness in their mind, and they need to go to a healing center to acquire a sense of wholeness. Others discover when they arrive that there are many areas of activity there in work, study, worship, entertainment—all of which mirror their counterparts on earth.

The Beyond is very different, though, in that everything is created by the power of thought. Souls move about through the power of thought too. To get from one place to another, they "wing the spirit," which is like traveling in a beautiful light of vibrating particles or impulses of electricity. When they do this, A.D. says, they look like Halley's comet as they soar through the air. Evidently the soul is an energy field, and from that field, through the power of thought, the soul can assume whatever form it wishes to take. Everything that is done has a purpose, however, for, whether on earth or in the heavenly planes, growth is the aim and object of existence.

One very evidential statement confirming A.D. as our communicator occurs in this chapter. He mentions that he has learned to enjoy the wonderful concerts in the realm beyond, and that on earth he had not fully appreciated what sustenance music gave to the soul. I had to smile when I heard that. Whenever my mother and I attended symphony concerts, we could never persuade him to come along. He wasn't in the least bit interested, and would always manage to find an excuse for staying home!

<hr />

WE CALL THE WORLD we find ourselves in immediately after death the "astral plane." From this point we can progress to higher planes—to higher levels of consciousness. By "higher" planes I do not mean spatially higher, but rather those planes that have a finer vibration.

All of the planes of consciousness have different frequencies of vibration. For instance, the matter of earth is composed of atoms and these atoms are composed of energy that vibrates. The matter of earth is denser than the matter of the higher planes. As you can see light waves that vibrate at a "visual observing" rate, so you can see the matter of earth. However, as you cannot see radio or television waves, which vibrate at too fast a rate to be seen, so you cannot see the matter of the world beyond, unless you are clairvoyant.

The spiritual bodies of those who have died vibrate at a rate too fast for your physical eyes to see, but they can be viewed by clairvoyants whose sight has been opened to receive this faster vibration. For example, if you look at an airplane propeller that is not in motion, you can see the blades. When that propeller is operating at full speed, though, the blades are spinning so fast that you can't see them—instead you see *through* them. Likewise, when the spiritual body leaves the physical body, it is vibrating at a rate too fast for your physical eyes to see.

The world beyond is not "up there" somewhere. It's *here*, a change of condition. All the different frequencies of vibration are in one space. It's rather like a big sponge that contains the different densities of water—soapy water, salt water, clear water. You can compare that to the different densities or vibrations I have here. I can be soapy water, and I can come down and see you. I can be salt water, and I can stop on the mind level. Or I can be clear water, and I can zoom through the mental plane, which is a plane of finer vibration than the astral plane, without any trouble at all.

I have taken a number of trips out into the mental plane, and it is most interesting. You get there before you know it, whereas in the astral plane you are conscious of your going. This is due to the difference in the rate of vibration of the two planes. For example, if you can send a thought around the world in no time at all, this can be compared to the mental plane. If you send a picture around the world, it takes longer than the thought, and this can be compared to the astral plane. In the astral body you are slower when you are moving, because you are moving through denser atmosphere—denser vibrations—but not as dense as the physical world.

The astral world, where we go immediately after death, is almost a replica of your world, except that it is of a finer substance. That's why when we step out of our physical body and arrive on the astral plane, all is familiar—it's a reflection of the earth plane. This gives us a sense of continuity. When people who are fearful of death and who are closely tied to their own home die, the transition to this plane is made easy by the fact that there is a replica of their own home here. That helps them to feel comfortable in the beginning. The thread of familiarity is there. They can adjust and work from that place as long as they need to. After that, it disappears, just disintegrates, because they don't need it anymore. Nothing remains in creation here if it is not needed. It then goes into the great Whole, so that the material may be used again.

There seems to be one universal temperature here—not hot, not cold. However, it is interesting to note that we can experience your weather on the physical plane. I can "sense" the cold and snow, frost in the air, and I can even see the crystals, Ruth. We can also sense the changes in the earth's atmosphere, whether heavy and damp, or light and dry.

When we arrive here, we are not expected to rearrange ourselves on our own. We have trained souls who are dedicated to work with the new arrivals, for we are in some ways strangers in a strange land. Certainly it is governed by different vibratory laws from the physical world we have left. We are indeed in a new area of feeling, and we need help and tender loving care. And, my goodness, we get it—richly overflowing love and care.

After our joyful reunion with loved relatives and friends, we are led away by our helpers to a place of healing. My room was filled with sunlight, and I was enfolded in soft floating bands of various colors. I have since been told that different colors are used for different people, depending on what type of healing is needed. I was conscious of healing hands removing tension and strain, producing a gradual sense of being more and more relaxed. All sense of time and pressure leaves us.

We float and we dream of music, and color, and soothing words, all of which produce meandering thoughts.

GROWTH CONTINUES

No one need be bored here. Growth is the aim and object of living, whether on earth or here in the heavenly planes. We are blessed because others who have traveled the road before us are ready to give us a helping hand.

Sometimes in the beginning, upon arrival here, a soul who has died from starvation needs to be fed, because his desire for food is so great. Such souls eat food, which we know is imaginary food, but they think it is tangible food. "Oh, how wonderful!" they say. "It's true then, that when you get to paradise there are feasts and we can be filled." This has to take place, and I've watched it happen. Eventually they will say, "Oh, we've eaten enough. Surely there must be something more to do besides this." They are then brought out and formed into groups and classes. Teachers and helpers teach them that the hunger is all in their mind, because they no longer have a physical body to feel hungry. This never impinged on me. As I functioned in my astral body, I was just very thankful that I didn't have to bother with food anymore. But there are souls who do need to go through this experience.

Those on earth who are bigoted or intolerant or self-absorbed find coming here to be a very painful and disturbing experience because they continue to think in their bigoted, intolerant, and self-centered way. They soon realize that they are quite uncomfortable and very lonely. It's almost as if they're encased in a hard shell or covering. They cannot begin to experience the joy and wonder of the life here until they learn to overcome these negative feelings that are retarding their spiritual growth.

When we are adjusted to the conditions on the astral plane, we generally prefer to continue with the life we have lived on earth, if we feel it has unfinished areas. That only applies to those who have enjoyed their careers. We know there are those who have faithfully earned a living in a trade or profession that was not satisfying. These persons absorb the knowledge gained, and then go on to become involved in studies or other areas of work they wish to explore. They are assisted in developing in new areas through the advice of others, by attending groups, or by going back to "college." Too easily, one might think that when we die we become clever, able to do anything we desire with ease. Not so. We work at it! Children who die young also grow and develop, just as they would on earth.

There are many areas of activity here in work, study, worship, entertainment—all areas that mirror earth activities. For example, we may attend a concert, a play, a ball game, an art gallery, or go to the magnificent Valley of Praise. The last is one of the most wonderful experiences one can imagine. Such sound—such colors!—so many beautiful people all raising their vibrations in songs of praise, accompanied by music from every instrument that has been used by man. One is just enfolded in the wonderful sounds. I had not related fully to the wonders of music when I was on earth. Feeling enfolded, colored, and expanded into at-oneness with musical sound was a new experience for me here. Now, with pleasure, I can devote time to listen and absorb, and I am thankful for that opportunity for growth. You may have happiness on earth, but you don't know what true happiness is until you come here.

THOUGHT IS THE CREATIVE POWER

One of the first lessons we learn is that here we are known for ourselves, and not for our possessions. If you have measured status by ownership of yachts, houses, cars, and other material things, it takes a while to release the yacht-house-car mentality. Here we use the creative power of thought to bring into being whatever we wish, whether it be clothes, a house, furniture, a garden—whatever we feel we need or desire. Thought is our motivating force. No engines, no windmills, nothing mechanical needs to be used. Thought is the creative power.

Cars or yachts or planes are not even needed, because we are taught to use our power of thought to "wing the spirit," and we travel instantaneously through space. Then we are in a beautiful light of vibrating particles or impulses of electricity, and we look like Halley's comet as we go through the air. This is a very interesting phenomenon. As you see it, you wonder, "Is that a man or a woman?" After being here a while you get so used to seeing it that you don't even bother to think about it.

Some laughable happenings can occur. I remember I was anxious to see my son soon after I "died," and before he died, which was not long after me. I thought about him and wondered how his teaching was progressing at the university in North Dakota. I linked in to earth time and decided Al would be free. I was rather laboriously planning my route, not realizing that I could simply link into his wave-broadcast. While I was thinking about my son, I suddenly thought about my daughter, Ruth, and I immediately found myself in *her* home in New York, where she was preparing a meal. I saw her, the phone rang, she moved body and thoughts, and I was left adrift. My Helper jolted my memory, and I then concentrated on my son, and suddenly found myself with *him* in North Dakota. Sharply focused thinking is vitally necessary here, so begin to train yourselves while still on earth. Scatterbrained folks have an even harder time here than on earth.

ARE THERE ANIMALS IN HEAVEN?

As animals exist on earth, so they also continue to exist in the spiritual realms. They retain the character they had on earth and enjoy our existence here. Loved animals await the arrival of their owners. There is not an immediate meeting, for when we first come here, there is a need for centering our thoughts and adapting. However, when we ourselves are feeling centered, then a joyous reunion with our pets takes place.

There are those here who love and understand animals, and who choose to give their time to care for the dogs or cats, or other pets, until their owners arrive. Margaret, your friend Doff is doing this. She has many dogs under her loving care.

Often, before we have died, we have been on the astral plane during our sleep state with our beloved pets who have died, so the connection has been kept. But it seems that if we had pets in our earlier days and have no longer shown an interest in them, and have not made an effort to seek them out, then these pets are enfolded and absorbed into the group soul of that category of animal. There is a dog group soul, a cat group soul, and separate ones for all species of animals, birds, insects, fish, and so on. There, the results of the experiences absorbed by every individual animal's core will be taken and added to the knowledge of the total group soul. In this way the level of intellect is enhanced, as are all instincts.

THE WORLD OF IDEAS

Now we see but a poor reflection as in a mirror; then we shall see face to face. Now I know in part; then I shall know fully, even as I am fully known.

1 Corinthians 13:12

Have you ever wondered how and why the same ideas seem to spring up all around us at the same time? They are showered down from the mental plane, where all creativity takes place. It is a plane of finer vibration. When A.D. is in his mental body, his vibrations are so fine that he can pass through the body of someone still on the astral plane.

In the Beyond, A.D. explains, thought forms are projected on the ether as pictures. Those on the mental plane communicate through thought alone, simply "tuning in" to the thoughts projected by others on the mental plane or on the astral plane.

❖

The other day, you wanted to know what I meant when I said that I put my astral body to sleep and went out onto the mental level. I'll give you an example.

Recently I visited a man who had been killed suddenly in a road accident. He's now here on the astral plane and very depressed. I talked with him and tried to comfort him. After he was taken away to a healing center to be treated, I returned to my favorite lake to sit by the water. There, I meditated about whether I had ministered to him in the proper way, and if I had really helped him. He'd been in a very shocked state, and I couldn't tell by the dull light in his eyes if I was getting through to him.

I was still meditating on the condition of this man the next day when, suddenly, there beside me on my right, a shaft of light came down. As I gazed at it, trying to see where it ended, a figure of light appeared. I realized that I could communicate with this being simply by thinking. This being said to me, "I have come to help you. You just wondered if what you said and did for that young man was a help. I have come to take you to him, so that you may see the results of what you did."

I stood up, and he said, "No, no. Just leave your astral body sitting there. I want you to think of yourself as light, and I want you to come with me in your light."

And as I thought of myself as light, it suddenly surrounded me. Enveloped in this light, I felt myself traveling very swiftly. I knew I was still *me*, but I was in that light.

Before I knew it, I was standing at the bedside of the young man. I looked at him, and he seemed very, very firm. However, when I put my hand on him—because I still seemed to have a body—my hand went through him. It gave me the oddest feeling! Then the voice in the light said to me, "He still has his astral body. You are in your mental body. Your vibrations are much finer than his."

I looked above the young man, and I saw patterns of color and rays of light, very tangible rays of light. It was explained to me that these were healing astral rays that were focused on his astral body, particularly on his legs. He had lost his physical legs in the accident, and the astral counterparts of those legs were more tenuous looking than the rest of his astral body.

Next, I looked up the length of his body to his head. It was surrounded by his thought forms, which were moving through him and around him.

"How do I interpret this?" I asked.

No sooner was the question posed than the answers came back. The day before, I had told the young man, "You are in safekeeping." Then, wishing to comfort him, I had added, "Yea, though I walk through the Valley of Death, I will fear no evil." Now, in the thought form around him, I saw a dark valley, but there were stars and there was a light. In his mind, the young man had pictured himself walking through a dark valley, a valley that he had walked through on earth as a child.

The voice said to me, "Now you see he found comfort in that. It was something he remembered."

I had also said the Lord's Prayer, hoping that its comforting universal message would get through to him. And now the next thought form I saw above him was a picture of a father holding his child, but it was not at all the heavenly Father that I had in mind. This young man was remembering his own father, a plump man who was still on earth. The boy was visualizing the way his father used to put his arm around him and say, "Come on, son, let's go and play ball." The memory was reassuring, because he felt very close to his father.

I told the being who was with me that I wanted to think about this a bit more, and he said, "Very well then, go back to where you came from. Be in your body."

"I want to go back to where I was," I said to myself. "I want to be in my body."

Immediately, I was back in my astral body, sitting beside the lake. As I sat there, I thought about the other things I'd said to the boy, and the moment I thought about him—whee-*wham*!—I'd gone, and I was back there with him. There I was! This happened three or four times.

This experience was of great value to me, because I realized then that this is how I travel in the mental body. I am now in a mental field. I am communicating without any thought of body. I am being just thought.

HOW THOUGHT FORMS INFLUENCE CREATIVE WORK ON EARTH

Sometimes when you on earth are concentrating intensely on something—profound problems or difficult mathematical equations, for example—suddenly you are not conscious of *you* anymore. You seem to be just the thought. If you can, try to recognize at that moment that you are then on the beltway of all thought and all thinking. Even in a physical body, one can be on the mental plane, in the world of thought. It is from that level that the great inspired ideas come down to earth.

Many ideas and inspirations never reach anybody on earth, because they are beyond the scope of the human brain. However, when there is a need to take humanity one step forward, or to educate people in a certain way, then there is a concerted effort for thought forms to be showered down. You may notice that suddenly there are many books on a new subject. That is because people have picked up on the new ideas coming down. It is from this world of ideas that one particular kind of architecture appears in many different areas at the same time, or new space vehicles are developed simultaneously. When people all around the world have the same idea, it is because each has received creative thought help from the world of ideas. *Nothing*, not a single thing, can be created unless it has already been created in the world of ideas. This is the creative aspect of God.

THE GROTTO OF EXPANDING
CONSCIOUSNESS

All you have made will praise you, O Lord;
your saints will extol you.

PSALMS 145:10

MANY OF US have experienced moments when the beauty of nature and sometimes even that created by men and women has taken us out of ourselves. Unfortunately, when they come at all, these moments are usually fleeting and often quickly forgotten. In the Beyond, there is a magnificent grotto, filled with the beauties of nature, art, and music, and tended by delightful beings most of us here have never realized actually exist.[8] Souls are taken there to experience and appreciate all the wonders of earth life and art, so that when they return again to earth, they will be more aware of the beauty and variety of creation.

Here, A.D. shares with us the incredible beauty of that grotto and the discoveries he made there about the meaning and purpose of our existence.

—◈—

ABOUT A YEAR after I arrived here, a group of us were taken on a boat trip to visit an underground grotto, or cave, in a mountain. We traveled on a narrow river that is not more than a mile wide at its broadest point. Our attention was directed to the hills that were on either side of us. For a while, there were trees all along the bank, and then we were out into the open. It was rocky country, and the vegetation and rocks blanketed the landscape with the most gorgeous heatherlike hues of purple, green, and mauve. We hadn't been gone very long—about ten minutes in your time—when we realized that we were coming to a wider stretch of land on the left-hand side. There we disembarked so that we could explore some grottoes in this magnificent mountain.

As we stepped out, an astonishing thing happened. I actually saw a gnome. What do think of that? *A gnome!* This little man had a brown beard and a pointed hat. He was plump, and he wore a belt around his waist. He was pushing a wheelbarrow that had some gardening tools in it, and he was tending the lichen and the plants that were growing on the rocks. All the time he was going along, he made a soft little noise between a whistle and a sigh in a tune of about three notes. He was walking along, keeping time to this tune. He smiled and waved, and then went to look at the flowers.

"Did you see that gnome?" I asked my companions.

"No, I can't say I *saw* anything," one man said, "but I did *hear* something."

A woman in front responded that there was a gnome, and he was wearing a green hat, a red jacket, and green trousers.

I thought to myself, "That's odd. I didn't notice the color of his clothes. I will have to become more observant."

The gnome appeared to be mixing a little into the landscape. I saw him as green, a little bit of brown, and a flash of red. And I could see *through* him—right to the rocks and the flowers behind him.

Then we came to the entrance of the cave. Inside it was light, and a warm breeze met us. It was rather like going into a big department store on a cold day and being greeted by a nice, warm current of air as you go through the doorway.

We were divided into groups, and a guide came forward to be with each group. Our party had a charming fair-haired lady. She wore a straight robe, which was the most beautiful pink and gold, shot through with colors that reflected and glittered and sent out sparkling rays. She said she would do her best to help us and to answer any questions we had. We were told that this grotto had been prepared for our study and growth. Appreciation of the beauties of life that it contained would enable us, when we returned to earth, to have a greater appreciation of the beauty of nature and human creativity. These were gifts of life that we hadn't fully recognized and been grateful for when we had physical eyes.

It struck me that this place was like a very long arcade or mall. Down the center were seats, beautiful flowers in pots, and pools with magnificent species of fish. The pools weren't set in the ground. They were just a little below eye level.

There were all sorts of alcoves, and the first one I was attracted to had water with the most gorgeous flowers growing in it. There were many little creatures of the sea in there also—all lit up, and so beautiful! This area of glass must have been twenty feet long and about as high. The sea creatures were many different shapes. They were iridescent, like phosphorus, and in the lower, deeper portion of the pool their lovely bodies flashed with brilliant lights. I stood there completely fascinated.

After a while, I moved a little farther on, to a very large area with high domes. There I found representations of the most beautiful sculpture and statues created throughout the ages. There was a replica of Michelangelo's David, and there was the Venus de Milo *with her arms*, and many other classical works. There were other areas where plants and trees were growing—and everywhere the sweetest fragrance perfumed the air.

EXPANSION OF CONSCIOUSNESS

As I waited for my group to join me, I was suddenly attracted to the other side, where there was a great deal of sound. I hesitate to call it music. It was a cacophony of tones. I walked across to it, and I could see nothing but colored columns, similar to organ pipes. There were pipes of all sizes—great big ones with holes in them, little tiny ones near the ground, and large ones up in the air—all forming an orderly picture and all emitting sound.

Never before had sound affected me as the tones from those pipes did. It seemed to me that each of the notes had a message. They were calling to me and starting to vibrate on and through my body. As they did, I began to feel very light, very uplifted and joyous. I could almost say *expanding* in consciousness. I looked at a man near me, and the pulsating light that was coming through from his form was truly amazing. I then looked at myself, and I was *growing and becoming*. I felt that all the things that weighed me down at times were being dispersed. I experienced a tremendous exultation.

When I felt this exultation, I didn't want to look at any of the others. I wanted to be alone. Suddenly, I sank through the floor, and I found myself inside a bubble of color. I couldn't see anybody else, and I wasn't conscious of whether there were any chairs, or whether I was in a hall. I was just in this bubble. It seemed to be in the place where the sound had come from, as if the sound was being created here and was going up through the pipes so the people up above could hear it and see the colors it produced. But the interesting thing was that while you were on the floor above and looking at other things, you weren't conscious of the sound. Only when you directed your attention toward it did you become aware of it.

Inside that bubble, I felt that I no longer had legs, arms, feet, or head. I became a sort of swinging or swaying vibration. My mind went back to a lecture I had attended on the negative and the positive—the yin and the yang. I realized that the forward and receding surges going through me could be called positive and negative surges.

Then I became aware of a voice, one that I have heard not only here but before I came here, when I prayed and received instruction or help. This voice said to me: "Be aware of yourself. Find *yourself*. Be aware of yourself—use yourself—the *true self*. Be aware of the pulsating life and the God that is within you. Don't feel that this is a discipline. Don't look upon this as a rule or a regulation or an order or a command, but be *aware*. Know that you are part of this great, universal, creative force and power, this God. Know and be aware."

Although when I was on earth there had been moments when I had sat quietly and been aware, the awareness I now experienced was magnified a thousand times. I began to feel that I no longer wanted to be A.D. I no longer had any desire to think in the way I'd been thinking. I just wanted to *know*. Somehow I understood that if I could *know*, then there should be no doubts. I don't think that I have been besieged by many doubts. Still, I must say that since I've been here, I had begun to think, "Well, now, what purpose can I fulfill while I'm over here? Am I growing? Am I just being the same person? And when I think back into A.D., am I bringing anything new to A.D.? Or am I just the same A.D. who had a physical body and walked around on two feet?" Suddenly I was aware that my searching thoughts had brought me to this point. Now I understand that this is one of the laws of the universe: As you think, so you are.

If you on earth say to yourselves, "I've come this far and now I want to be different. I want to change. I want to be better. I want to see clearer. I want to know more deeply. I want to have understanding." If you send out these thoughts, it may seem that nothing happens. However, there *will* come a time when a directive arrives. Perhaps you'll experience it during a period of meditation.

And so now I have received my directive here: *Become aware.*

THE SECRET OF INSPIRATION

"So I say to you: Ask and it will be given you; seek, and you will find; knock, and the door will be opened to you."

LUKE 11:9

FROM TIME TO TIME, we have all experienced a jolt of inspiration. Though it fires up our mind, it seems to surge through our body too, giving us renewed energy to act upon our new understanding. A.D. has discovered that inspiration can also be felt in the astral body. And now that he is in the Beyond, he has learned the secret of its source, which he shares with us.

He has also discovered the important role music can play in making us open to inspiration, and he tells us what he observed during services at my church and during a concert by the Westchester Symphony Orchestra that Margaret and I and our friend Mary Louise attended. My husband, Hal, played double bass with that orchestra.

While A.D. was talking with us about inspiration, Margaret received a "picture" of him and his surroundings. When he left, she described what she saw, and I'd like to share that with you. It is in italics at the end of this chapter, following the ornament at the end of A.D.'s discussion.

INSPIRATION IS WHAT occurs when we suddenly see a familiar thought or subject in a new light that makes it shine through to us with renewed understanding. Just as you can experience inspiration in the physical body, so, too, can I experience it here in my astral body. I see now that inspiration emanates from the Holy Spirit. I am inspired. I am enlightened. I am lit up. Facts that I may already know can be illumined and transformed.

Through the light of inspiration you place a fact in a different context, and you clothe it in different words. You make a different picture of it, and this picture will reach out and be a source of comfort and help—even *inspiration*—to somebody who listens to your presentation of this fact.

Saint Paul has presented a text. At the time he gave that text he was presenting what he knew, having received that knowledge through inspiration. In the same way now, we in the clergy will take a text, read what other people have thought about it, and then we'll look at it again and suddenly *we* will see it in another light. The Holy Spirit illumines that light for our understanding. This is the great difficulty with translating thought to other people. We have to give according to our understanding, and that understanding may change hour by hour, or day by day, or month by month. In stodgy people, it may even take years. Whatever time it takes, the change is produced by inspiration.

More and more I have come to appreciate music as a vehicle of inspiration. This morning I attended the service at your church, Ruth. As the music of that service reached the congregation, I saw that it was a source of inspiration for about sixty percent of the people.

Last night I went along to the symphony concert with you. I stood behind Hal as he played the double bass. I watched the audience and the patterns that the music built, and it was fantastically beautiful. Then I went to where you were sitting, Ruth, and stood behind you and saw how you were receiving it. Next, I stood behind Margaret, and then Mary Louise, and I was able to see how they responded. It was obvious that the three of you were finding a unison with one another through that music.

I moved to others. With some, I could see that they were there only because they wanted to be seen—it's the "proper" thing to do. One man was thinking, "Why can't I improve my golf by doing such-and-such? So-and-so does such-and-such, and he doesn't slice his ball. Tomorrow I'll call him up, and we'll go out..."—*Clap, clap, clap! Very good, very good!*—He looks at his wife, who is thoroughly enjoying the music, but she is also thinking about her hairdresser and what she's going to say to her.

You know, when you are released from the physical body and you see people, it can be a bit of a shock. When you're in the physical body, you're seeing through a glass darkly. Even if you're a clairvoyant, you see it only partially. But when you come over here and you *see*, you are somewhat shattered by what you see inside many people. They render lip service and they render a mind service, but neither has anything to do with their God service. You even see people working in reverse. You think to yourself, "Dear God, what on earth can you *do* with that person?" Sometimes I wonder why those shining ones—or whatever we like to call those beings who are looking down and observing us—I wonder why they don't weep. They don't weep, because they know that eventually all will be well. And this is the thought that I am trying to hang on to.

So many people today go through the motions of just making a grimace, a pretend smile. You wish to goodness that they hadn't bothered. There is a terrible pain that comes when you see the way some people are. While you may sense it when you're on earth, and may feel distressed over it, it is so much more noticeable when you are here and released from the physical body.

But there is *hope*, and this is what I really want you to know this morning. There is hope. This is what we have to get through. We all have to understand that the Power is there for the asking. The Holy Spirit is with us. It is in us and around us. But we need to be open to that Power. Inspiration will come to ùs to guide us on the right path, but only if we are open and ask.

I'm going to leave you now, and the Lord be with you.

⎯◆⎯

Margaret received a "picture" of A.D. as he talked, and when he left, she described what she saw:

I saw A.D. just now. He's walking toward what seem to be rose beds, and he has come from what looks to me like an arbor. It's circular and it has pillars, rather like the Greek temples. It's not a very large place. There's room for about six or seven chairs. He seems to have been sitting on a white wrought-iron chair with patterns on it. Much of the time he sat on that chair he had his elbows on his knees and his chin in his hands, and he was looking down at a mosaic floor with many colors. The patterns of the floor keep changing, rather like a kaleidoscope.

Today A.D. is wearing a white short-sleeved shirt, white shoes, and what we call in England white flannel tennis trousers. There were three other people with him, but not your mother. I saw your mother come through an arbor a little distance away, and she was carrying an armful of roses. When he left, he walked toward her. They met by those rose beds, and now they're going off together.

THE ASTRAL TEMPLE
OF REJUVENATION

How lovely is thy dwelling place, O Lord Almighty!
PSALMS 84:1

MUCH OF A.D.'S TIME on earth was spent in working with the underprivileged and advocating for human rights. He never forgot that it was God's work he was doing as well as his own, and, deeply devoted to his religion and mission as a minister, he always made time for prayer and meditation. Here he describes an astral temple where he and others in the Beyond find strength and renewal. And he reveals a pleasant surprise: Many of us in this world find strength and renewal there too.

❖

THE OTHER DAY I let Margaret see the temple that I often visit over here. It is a replica of a Chinese temple that was set in the mountainous country that separates Tibet and China. This temple is not only for those of us on the astral plane. It is also for you on earth. Both of you, and many others from the physical plane, have visited it. Sometimes at night, when you are asleep and you come here, you use it for renewal and rejuvenation.

The temple is set down in a court with many trees and benches and other places to sit. It has a wide veranda and the most beautiful jade-green tiled roof. Its wide eaves have little wild creatures and birds and squirrels and fish carved on their ridges.

One never knows whom one will meet here, because if you stand and look at the temple with psychic eyes, you will see many, many threads of light. These threads of light are pulsating with energy, with vibrations that are like telegraph wires that hum in the wind. On earth, when you walk along a road with telegraph wires, you can hear them singing. It's something like that.

I like to compare the threads that we see here in the astral temple to the thread that keeps one telephone in contact with another. Once you have been here, the thread that you leave between you and this place remains intact. It can be seen going backward and forward. There are times when you may sit down for a minute and say, "Oh, I'm tired, I must relax." You may not consciously think of this temple—you may not consciously think of anything. But because you have been here and left behind your stamp, there is renewal that comes down to you from here.

Don't think that you come here just once, and then the thread of your presence here is broken. Your imprint remains on the ether. No one can go anywhere and not leave his or her imprint, not still have a contact. Now you can understand how important it is to choose wisely the places you visit. You don't want to be connected to too many places. That is why some people always want to take their vacations in the same place: They get a strong sense of comfort and belonging from having established binding ties there.

REINCARNATION

"But I tell you, Elijah has already come, and they did not recognize him, but have done to him everything they wished...."

MATTHEW 17:12

THROUGHOUT HIS LIFE, A.D. was intrigued by the concept of reincarnation. We had often discussed it, and he thought that it would clarify some passages in Scripture—for example, Matthew 17:9–13, quoted in part above; Mark 8:27–29 and 9:11–13; and John 9:1–3.[9]

An article in *Reader's Digest* about the possibility of reincarnation also greatly interested A.D. It was about a young girl in India who visited a village she had never set foot in, yet she knew every street and building, and even recognized some of the inhabitants. It was suggested that she had lived there before, died, reincarnated, and returned. A.D. felt that could be a plausible explanation for this unusual story.

From the beginning of A.D.'s communications from Beyond, I have listened intently for any insights he could give us on the subject. Many have come through. We didn't include any of the earliest communications on reincarnation in *Witness from Beyond*, because A.D. wished it to be a handbook on the concept of survival after death and he didn't want material in it that might confuse his message.

Fascinating communications that touch on the subject have continued over the years, and it's now time to share them. In this chapter, I have included some of A.D.'s earliest references to reincarnation. Here, though he never studied in England during his life as A.D., he refers to having been taught Christianity in England. His description of helping souls "back down to earth," and his reference to life on earth being a "ladder of growth," are further indications of his early discoveries about reincarnation.

<hr />

ASSISTANCE TO SOULS
DESTINED FOR EARTH

I HAVE HAD SEVERAL interesting contacts here with my brother Karl, but his field of work is completely different. He is primarily concerned with assisting highly developed souls leaving the earth. I think that eventually my own main interest is going to be not in helping those who have just left the earth, but in helping those who are going back down to earth. My knowledge of earthly conditions is fresh enough in my mind to be of help in training some of those souls.

At the moment, I'm not able to do a great deal in that area because I am not yet able to raise my vibrations to get to the top of the curve of souls traveling toward earth. I have to catch them at the bottom of the curve, before they slip in. Right now, I'm in contact with those who are just beginning their descent at about the second or third month of pregnancy.

Eventually, I hope to be able to work with souls for two or three years before they even start their way down. That means that I have to expand myself in consciousness, and I have to learn how to adjust my still somewhat earthly vibrations to the tentative, slender vibrations that those souls function in at that time. It is quite fantastic, the schooling and instruction that the soul passes through before it goes into the black tunnel—into the void of going down to earth.

Margaret, your daughter was right when she said that she thought that you go down a long, long while in a tunnel, and when you wake up, you're there and you cry. You cry because you've lost the comfort of the darkness of the tunnel and your close contact with the guardian angels who are bringing you down.

SIMON THE ZEALOT

You are interested, Margaret, in Simon the Zealot. I will see if I can find any more information. It is true that he has been an inspirer of yours, and you *did* know him long ago, when you lived in Glastonbury. And it is true that he was martyred at Colchester. Someday, when you are going through Colchester, I will try to take you right to the spot where it happened. It's a marshland, down near the river. You see, I have been doing a little checking around in England, which was once my great love. That's because it is where I was taught much of my own Christianity. But that's another chapter, and for another day.

AWARENESS OF PAST INCARNATIONS

One day I heard Margaret say that George Bernard Shaw said he didn't mind the thought of survival if he didn't always have to be George Bernard Shaw. Well, first of all, I've not made a contact with dear G.B.S., but I can thoroughly agree that I don't want *always* to be saddled with A.D.'s personality. It's very useful at times, but just a little crusty on the edges, a little hidebound and restricting.

This will probably surprise you, but I have learned that I can draw on some aspects of personalities that I have used in former incarnations. To me, this is the biggest proof of reincarnation that I have found. I may now know in my new awareness who I was in ancient

Greece, for instance, or what I thought as a poor little monk scrubbing floors and trying to please all the big, pompous monks.

These portions of my personality, which are in the inner me, form part of my ego—if we use the term *ego* to mean the inner self. I may find those personalities in the depths of thought, and I may now use some of the personality traits that are stronger than those in the A.D. personality that died in 1970.

I find that the personality I have with me now as A.D. is a bit cumbersome, and I want to refine it. My teachers assure me that, as time goes on, I may eradicate many of the aspects of A.D. that I don't particularly like and put them into a composite personality with all the others. Evidently, I'm going to be allowed to function in the A.D. personality *here*, but I'm not quite sure what I'm going to do with it when I leave here. It seems that I will have to hang it on the rack, as it were, and go down with another personality. I hope that the Lord will see fit to let me have a less clumsy body, and a little finer intellect, and a more humane approach to myself.

Ruth, you can't appreciate the battles I had when I was a young man. You saw some of the Armageddons I had as a grown man. But nobody else can fully appreciate the scars, or understandings, or aversions, or likes, or dislikes, or antipathies, or hatreds, or loves that another person winds up with after waging his individual life battles. It must have been very much easier for me to have been a more serene person in China, perhaps, or in Tibet, at a time when those civilizations had a more tranquil environment. Now, with all the buffeting the human race experiences on the planet, we have to be much stronger. We have to struggle to be more secure, more God-centered, more universally centered.

A VISIT TO THE DEEP SOUTH

Today I went to the Deep South with a group of men and women who had been Salvation Army officers on earth. We visited a corps of black

Salvation Army workers who were conducting a service of praise in Mississippi. It has been a long time since I've heard such wonderful singing. A tremendous volume of sound came from those forty to fifty people in their witness for the Lord.

The service was held in the open air and accompanied by music from a portable organ. The group sat side by side on benches and swayed together, and they stood up and sang. They prayed aloud, and there were many hallelujahs and shouts of "praise the Lord!". It was tremendously uplifting for me. It was the first time since my arrival here that I've seen anything like it. I received a large store of strength through what I felt and I saw there.

While I listened, I wondered, "Was I ever a preacher of the gospel in a colored body, in a country where it was very hot, and where I sweated and labored, and where the people sang and cried as they shouted for joy in their singing?" I felt a surge of excitement in my spirit as a distant echo inside me responded that this could have been so. I am beginning to realize that there are certain aspects of my personality that could have come not only from my parents, but also from my having been in other situations in other places at a previous time.

I'm told that I must be very careful not to let this become too much of a curiosity for me. Otherwise, these communications to you will not be cohesive and a proper continuous experience. If I am sharing the experiences of A.D. in the world beyond in 1971, I mustn't allow myself to go back and be A.D. as he was in 1870 or 1715. This is something I must remember, but it is difficult not to have flashbacks.

THE BIBLE AND THE PARANORMAL

When I was on earth as A.D. the pastor, people would tell me that they had reservations about getting involved with the paranormal. They felt it might be a bit evil, or the work of the devil. If they had read their Bible carefully, they would have found that it tells of many paranormal happenings. Nobody bothered to talk much about them in biblical times, because such happenings were taken for granted. Back then, people also took for granted that you live on after you die, and they believed in reincarnation too. I have a strong suspicion that as time went on, this person or that person would say when the Bible was read, "That idea doesn't really appeal to me—I just won't discuss it. I'll leave that little bit out." In that way, views presented about the Bible were narrowed.

I base my present thinking on the way my mind worked when I was A.D. on earth. I'm not yet distanced enough to discard much that I thought back then. I'm the sum total of my life and thoughts as A.D., plus some that I have gathered from other lives.

The time may come when I will no longer be concerned much about the way things are going on earth. I may be concerned only with the spiritual and mental development of those living there. But to do that, I will have to draw further away and become less emotionally attached to the earth. That's very difficult for me, because I really love earth's natural beauty.

Maybe I will never draw completely away. I may be one of those who will feel the call to stay near the earth. I may come back and come back and come back, and decide that I don't ever want to go and live on Venus or on any of the other planets, or in any of the other heavens.

It's too close to my sloughing off my physical body for me to be able to be sure about whether I'll return. One of these days I'll know, and I'll tell you. I may return later in a yellow, brown, or black body, depending on where I'm called to serve. It doesn't mean that I'll lose contact with my family or those I love, because love is a continuous joining. When you love someone, you can never cut the connection between you. You can never disconnect the plug or turn your back. The connection is always there.

THE LADDER OF GROWTH

Life on earth can be compared to a ladder of growth. The inner self takes on a different personality for each incarnation. The life then experienced is lived in steps of growth, which can be compared to climbing a ladder from bottom to top. When you get to the top of the ladder at the end of life, you do not step out into nothingness, since that ladder has always been supported by the reality that lies beyond. You simply step off the top rung and into your new mode of existence on the astral plane.

REVIEWING THE PAST LIFE

Do not be deceived: God cannot be mocked. A man reaps what he sows.

GALATIANS 6:7

LIFE IS A PROCESS of growth and development toward spiritual oneness with God, and each incarnation we experience on earth is an important step in that process. Some people may make a great deal of progress in a lifetime. Others may simply mark time while they live. Still others may actually regress. All of us, however, face a long review of our life when we move on to the heavenly realms after death.

We are the ones who conduct our review, and the lessons we learn from it are added to the core of our being. We must judge ourselves in total objectivity, and in doing so, we enter our own Heaven or Hell.

A.D. takes us through the review process here, and he urges us to examine our life every day while still on earth. This can greatly reduce the amount of review necessary after we die, and it will also help us to live a more Godly life while still in the physical body. He reminds us to use the Prophet Amos's plumb line[10] as a measure for our attunement to God and His purposes. The mention of Amos is also evidential of A.D. as our communicator. Amos was one of A.D.'s favorite prophets, and A.D. based many lessons on his teachings.

Our Soul, or Ego, is a compound of all our experiences. You on earth add to that core of knowledge continually, and so do all of us in the Beyond. Here, immediately after leaving our physical body, we begin reviewing our past life. Then we dissect the knowledge we've gained and add it to the core of our being. The process takes time, and we can undertake this very important part of the chain of our lives only with the valuable assistance of specially trained helpers who work with beings called the Lords of Karma. (These beings are more invisible than others, sensed but not seen. The sight of them would be overpowering to most of us.)

At the time of our review, we are disconnected from all of you. Our helpers teach us to stand aside, reverse gears, and go back over our life experiences from the last to the first. All are viewed objectively. We "live" through experiences, feeling happiness, sorrow, remorse—the whole gamut of emotions. Actions that produced positive results bring us a sense of happiness, or Heaven. Actions that produced negative results bring us pain, or Hell. Each of us inflicts Hell upon himself or herself.

There is no room here for hatred, malice, or the undermining of others we meet, who, like us, are part of God's creation—for God is Love. The only way to remove the painful obstruction that the hell of negative emotion puts in our way is to ask for revelation. We must seek out the Divine Law, and learn how to put ourselves into the Way of Divine Love. *Then* we find Heaven.

If we have harmed anyone in any way, our helpers assist us in receiving forgiveness and erasing past mistakes. We must always remember that we are adding to our soul's growth by positive "knowing." We must release negative thoughts and clear away the many "blocks" that have given us trouble in our life on earth, and this needs to be done thoroughly. For this reason, the review isn't rushed and can be interrupted by listening to lectures, to talks, to concerts, even by conversations with relatives and friends.

Eventually we reach the point at which we can assess and judge our life before the Higher Souls who are Teachers or Healers. They are not there to judge us, but to help us judge ourself. It can be months or years before our review is completed. It would be too overwhelming to do it all at once, so we are given time to absorb what we are learning. This enables us to apply our new knowledge in a positive way.

Review is our judgment, our "purgatory." We are all a "spark of God," and it is that spark—some call it conscience—that judges us. Until we can get on the right path, we really can't experience the true joy of Heaven, which God intends for us all. Through review, we learn how to order our lives in accordance with God's will. The Prophet Amos's plumb line is a measure for you on earth, and for us here.

During our review we are also shown how our experiences link with circumstances in previous lives. Karma, the Law of Cause and Effect, can never be avoided. "You reap as you sow" has been in the law of life since the beginning.

PRACTICE REVIEW WHILE STILL IN THE PHYSICAL BODY

If you who are incarnate would review every day while still on earth, it could greatly reduce the amount of review necessary after you come here. You will find that it is also extremely beneficial for living a God-centered life.

Practice going over each day's activities before retiring at night. This will help you keep a sense of Divine Order in your life. If you make amends while still in the body, it will diminish your regrets after you join us here. You will feel a sense of buoyancy from all the wonderful experiences of a God-centered day, and that will give you a positive outlook as you retire and prepare for the day to come.

Life is never monotonous. Keep in mind that though today you understand only a certain amount, tomorrow you will find your horizons spreading, opening out into new and fascinating vistas for growth.

BALANCING REGRETS
THROUGH SERVICE TO OTHERS

"...[S]erve one another in love."
GALATIANS 5:13

POSITIVE ACTION IS the key to a soul's progress in the Beyond. A.D. explains that the remorse we experience after our life's review can be lessened and eventually overcome through service to others. There are many services that can be rendered to others in the Beyond, and he describes two very special areas of assistance. One is working with people who have committed suicide, whose heavier vibrations keep them closer to earth until the time of their natural death arrives. The other is entering the "depths of hell" to minister to souls who have led depraved lives and to help them grow toward the realm of light.

———◆———

RELIVING OUR PAST life through intensive review enables us to prepare for our service to others here. That service helps us to balance our regrets, and it cleanses us of the dregs of our negative acts. For example, there is a man here who was a teacher of languages on earth. He was a rather self-centered individual, which he now deeply regrets.

Here, he is helping people who were not able to do well with languages on earth, for there seems to be a need in some persons to conquer such deficiencies before they can move on to the realm of pure thought. By dedicating himself to helping others in these areas, this teacher is, in turn, helping himself to become more selfless. Do you see what I mean?

The many areas of service are too numerous to cover, but I want to mention two of the very special ones that are devoted to assisting souls in the lower astral states progress toward, and eventually into, the realm of light.

Persons who commit suicide before the time they are meant to die find themselves in a state of heavier vibrations and closer to the earth than those of us who died natural deaths. They remain in this state of density until the time when they would have died naturally. They then may pass into the planes of finer vibration. There are those from the higher planes who dedicate themselves to helping these people grow spiritually during the period of waiting.

There is also a condition here that has been called the "depths of hell." When they die, people who have deliberately chosen to live debased and cruel lives, and have turned their backs on the light of God, find themselves in a state similar to groping in a dark and depressing fog. Everyone there is wrapped up in his own cruel thinking. These souls wander around in this lost state until they, of their own volition, make an attempt to turn toward the realm of light. Some may be lost for eons.

There are souls here who dedicate themselves to going into this dark realm and bringing spiritual light. The souls who are dedicated to this work of rehabilitation are protected by a spiritual covering, which wards off harm from the daggerlike thoughts of hatred thrown out by those in the dark realms. These ministers of light are not allowed to talk with these people. They stand nearby and call to them through thought—and prayer. The moment souls in this dark area respond in a positive way, the ones who have come to help are able to bring them out into a less dense foggy world, and eventually out into the realm of light.

THE AKASHIC RECORDS

Even now my witness is in heaven...

JOB 16:19

IN THE BEYOND there is a huge research library that contains the records of all our past lives. A.D. tells us that the repository where these Akashic Records are kept is unlike any library on earth, for our past-life information is stored on the ether. Permission is needed to study these records, and souls are allowed to do so only if it will help in their current spiritual growth.

———◆———

WE ARE NOT PERMITTED to see another person's thread of past lives unless that person gives us permission. But we can apply to see our own past lives if that knowledge will aid us in our spiritual growth. I went to the area here, a sort of massive research library, that contains the Akashic Records. When reviewing a past life, this is the source of all information. It is a repository of everything that has ever been, and I wanted to see if I could trace my lives in past civilizations in order to better understand the turmoil that is going on in various parts of the world today.

This repository is a veritable storehouse, holding the events of all the lives we have lived. The pattern of each life is "on record" on a special wavelength that is stored on the reflecting ether. When you on earth sit with one who is truly skilled in contacting your past lives, it is from this level that the information is culled.

As I look back on my incarnations, it is like reading a file of light— a long, trailing stream of light. Some incarnations show up like very nice pearls, but some seem to have bits of stone on them. I asked if I could go back and see my development in succeeding incarnations on this line, and I was told No. Previous reviews of each incarnation have placed the important lessons learned from those lives in the core of my being, and reanalyzing them in depth would be a waste of precious energy. I am given further deep insight into only those past lives that will help me in my spiritual growth at the present time.

In reviewing an incarnation just past, we are frequently shown how particular experiences in that incarnation link with circumstances in previous lives. When I entered incarnation as A.D., my goal was to work for God's Kingdom—to open doors, to educate others, and to work as I was ordained. And this is still my road here—to continue to educate, to advise, to learn more and to teach again. I am fortunate that my last two lives were preparations for the work I am doing here.

THE SOUL'S JOURNEY

O God, you are my God,
earnestly I seek you;
my soul thirsts for you...

PSALMS 63:1

WHAT IS THE SOUL? Philosophers, clergy, and ordinary people have been intrigued by that question through the ages. Now that he is in the Beyond, A.D. has discovered the answer, and he shares it here with us. It is not as simple as we might have hoped, but it is awesome and fascinating. Our soul is the intangible uniqueness that makes each one of us different. It consists of vibratory essences that serve as the vehicle for the Seed Atom, which is the part of us that returns to earth for subsequent lives. Every soul is permeated by the Divine Spark of God, which links us all to our Creator, and which prompts our quest for perfection so that eventually we can be at one with God.

A.D. explains that the soul vibrates at different speeds on the different planes of existence. Here, on the physical plane, the vibrations are slow. In the Beyond, the vibrations increase as one ascends to the higher levels. It is the soul that creates one's physical and personality image there, but the process changes as one moves from plane to plane. In the higher dimensions, souls are usually recognized by their thought patterns, which are as distinctive there as fingerprints are here. There are occasions, though, when some physical attribute may be needed for recognition, and A.D. explains how the soul works to manifest it.

The soul's final state of existence is to be merged into at-oneness with God the Creator, and even then it does not lose its own identity. But before that happens, many souls, seeking perfection, choose to return to earth for additional incarnations, and A.D. describes how that decision is made and prepared for.

As A.D. was communicating all this, he was sending Margaret images to help her understand the concept of the changes the soul goes through as it ascends the levels of the Beyond. "First I saw an astral figure," she told me. "That soon disappeared. Then I saw the etheric, which was more shapeless. Only the face was left, and then that disappeared. After that, there was just a face with a light around it. And then that went into an oval, and with an effort, A.D.'s face came again. Now that he's functioning mostly on the mental level, he won't project anything to me but his face, because that's how I know him. Actually, I recognize A.D. by his eyes even more than by his face. He has very compelling and expressive eyes."

Margaret said that though A.D. has moved on to the mental and spiritual planes, he continues to come close. "That's because he's serving in a more finite way. He is not out there looking down at us objectively. He comes nearer, and is deliberating what to say to us that can help us with our daily lives. There is a tremendous aura around A.D. It is predominantly orange/pink, since he loved all people, and still does."

That concern for humanity is certainly apparent here in the care he has taken to explain the workings of the soul and the preparation for new incarnations.

WE CANNOT *be*, *know*, and *do* everything in one lifetime. The part of us that returns for life after life is the Seed Atom. It has as its vehicle the vibratory essences we call the Soul. This is what on earth we refer to as our *Me* or our *Ego*. These are the vibrations that make each of us unique, and the Divine Spark of God permeates them. No two Egos are alike in any way except that the Divine Spark is in each. Every human being is a part of God, the Universal Creator of All. We must remember that our Inner Being, our Soul or Ego, doesn't change with death. Its ever-seeking quest for perfection—for at-oneness with God our Creator—continues.

Think of the soul as an energy field that vibrates at different speeds in the different dimensions of existence. In the physical dimension—your dimension on earth—it functions at its slowest speed. In the astral dimension, it is faster. The mental dimension is faster than the astral, and the mental/spiritual dimension is faster yet. The vibrations in human souls are different from the vibrations of angels, for angels are a different category of the creation.

It's only on the astral plane that we in the Beyond continue to show ourselves with a body and a personality, because without these, nobody would know us. We do this through the power of thought. To understand the process, think of the soul as a steady flame that coats the mind. It is from that soul-flame that we create a picture of our eyes or face, or even assume a whole clothed body. All this is done through thought alone, for thought is the basis of all creative power.

In the higher dimensions, we are usually recognized by our thought patterns. Distinctive patterns can never change until another incarnation. Canon West was right when he wrote in his foreword to *Witness from Beyond* that he recognized people by their thought form.

When we function in the mind dimension, we function in a wider area than we do on the astral or physical planes. The part of us we use is actually smaller, though, since we are vibrating at very high speed. In the mind dimension we assume the shape of a flame.

When we function in the spiritual body on the highest vibration that we can reach without merging ourselves into the Divine, we look like a gaseous light. Then we have to make ourselves a face or a hand or a voice to be recognized. But these come out of this gaseous light.

If I am functioning on the mental/spiritual level and want to contact you, I have to make myself compact and clothe myself in a protective etheric wrapping to wing my spirit onto the physical plane. Because of the speed at which I must travel, I need to keep this protective clothing around me. That etheric wrapping around the mind is shaped like a tulip. You perhaps just see a light in the corner of the room. That's when I come just as light, and the thought I bring comes in and out of that light. That's why a clairvoyant may say, "All I see are waves and globes of light."

Here, when we develop the ability to know each other by our thoughts and not our looks, we are functioning in the mind/spirit body. But the soul is still there, because you do need the vehicle of the soul to function as a distinct individual. You never leave your soul-body until you are ready to merge into the Divine. Even then, you would not lose total comprehension of yourself, but you would no longer consider returning to earth again as a separate individual. This would be a final state of existence—being enfolded into at-oneness with our Creator God.

Often, however, another life is desired to test again one's strengths and weaknesses. Some souls remain close to earth, because they need to return to assist others, or to repay others who helped them. Many such desires are expressed, but generally the decision is to wait awhile, to consolidate, to learn, to renew contacts, to study, to help others here, and to experience fully the wonderful aspects of *being* where we are now. Only afterward do we begin the lengthy planning for return to earth.

The hierarchies of Saints, Angelic Beings, Leaders, Helpful Guides, "Judges," and their Helpers are there for us. We can, with their assistance, eventually decide that we will return to earth, and that decision initiates activity. One's choice of sex can vary from incarnation to incarnation, depending on where and how one is to serve. The education for the return begins on all levels, and it may involve "years" of preparation. We have our own Higher Beings who help us in this preparation. These beings have been with us since we began. I guess they get tired of our slipups now and then, but they never decry our efforts. They have boundless faith and love, and they always lend an attentive ear and a helping hand.

It's an interesting fact that most persons can grow faster spiritually while incarnate. The incarnate energy is denser. That makes it more possible for you, while embodied in flesh on earth, to take hold of a particular problem area and shape it into a more constructive pattern. Your period of incarnation on the physical plane is thus a very important period of education. It contributes to your own spiritual evolution and that of all humanity. You can elect not to return, and many do, after they have achieved a certain spiritual development. But the physical plane is a "school" for learning and development, and so most souls do desire to return for a series of incarnations.

THE PROCESS
OF INCARNATION

In his hand is the life of every living creature and the breath of all mankind.

JOB 12:10

EVERYONE WONDERS HOW the process of incarnation takes place. Margaret and I became even more curious about it when her daughter was expecting her first child. A.D. was drawn in for that significant event in Margaret's life, and he observed the actual process. He also studied a number of other pregnancies and births, and he told us what he had learned from them about the various stages of the soul's involvement in the formation of the fetus. This topic has such far-reaching implications that I asked A.D. on three different occasions to share his observations. Each time his descriptions and explanations were virtually identical.

In his account that follows, A.D. takes us on the soul's journey from the higher realms to begin a new life here on earth. He tells us about the special care that is given to the soul and to the prospective mother. And he describes that beautiful and awesome moment at which the soul enters the fetus and life begins. He also brings a message of solace to parents who have lost a child—and a somber warning to all of us about making the world a welcoming place for our children.

CONCEPTION, THE UNION of two cells, instantly sends out a note and a light to the spiritual realm, so that a soul wanting to come to earth is attracted toward that union. In some cases, the soul may have been attracted to those potential parents before. Immediately, a subtle connection is made by the soul with the aura of the mother, and the Angels of Form begin to work on the higher planes to prepare for the entry of the soul into the fetus.

As I've told you before, there are creative beings from the higher realms who make the preparations required to bring a new life into being. The subtle replicas of the physical body are created for each of the higher planes, and the soul is prepared, in advance of birth, to adjust to incarnation.

When the fetus quickens, the incoming soul seems to become more closely attached to the aura of the mother, but it does not actually enter the physical body at that time. The soul does not actually enter the physical body until the moment of birth.

Through observations I have made in the delivery rooms of hospitals at the actual time of birth, I have seen with my own eyes the descending souls with their accompanying retinue of Light Beings. Every incarnating soul is carefully escorted into the denser atmosphere. Wrapped in garments of strength and purity, the souls come "down" on beams of light—blue, or green, or gold, or pink. All are enclosed in protective armor of shimmering gold.

Just before birth, one can observe the guardian from the higher realms holding what appears to be the spiritual replica of the baby, which shines with the energy and Light of the ego enclosed inside. At the moment of birth we see this spiritual form, held in the hands of the guardian, lowered and placed above the mother. Suddenly it disappears and merges with the physical, and the child cries.

The soul actually appears to enter the physical body when the baby takes its first breath. After the birth, we see the physical body as a gray form, and the light form, which had been held above the mother, can be seen emanating from within and penetrating the physical form.

If a fetus is aborted in the second or third month of pregnancy, it appears that the in-coming soul has not yet drawn close enough to the auric field of the mother to be too adversely affected. Since it may not even be aware of the fact, the disruption is not as drastic as some people believe. However, when you abort a fetus at any point after conception, you are really contravening the creative laws of the universe. You are interrupting a creative process that has been set in motion on many levels. If you destroy a body that could be used for an in-coming soul, that soul is deprived of opportunity, and the mother, also, is often left with a debilitating sense of frustration. I would certainly not advocate abortion as a routine method of population control. Family planning should be by birth control before conception, by not starting the creative process in the first place.

There is a special group of volunteers here who devote themselves to caring for certain incarnating souls and their mothers. They know that these in-coming souls are only going to touch earth and then die and come back, perhaps only drift into the body and then out again. Such souls need very particular care when they are brought away again from the earth. They must not be snatched back, but have to come back very slowly, almost as slowly as they go down. They cannot leave suddenly because they have not yet taken on another personality, and so they have no outer crust or shell. Canopies of various colors of light are provided to protect these souls who are returning to the spiritual realms. It is extraordinary, the different ways in which souls are met and helped and looked after.

Careful attention is also given to all potential mothers, because every woman who loses her baby at birth needs special treatment with very special rays of light. Quite different rays of light are placed around women who have an abortion because they have conceived a child under conditions that don't allow it to come to be born. The women whose health doesn't permit them to continue pregnancy or who yearn for a child and then it dies at birth need treatment with one type of healing rays of light. The girl who conceives a child on a spree, or while she's on drugs, and then says "I don't want it! I can't have it!" is treated with very different rays. Just as there are varieties of souls who come and there are varieties of reasons for conception, there are varieties of healing power for those various situations when a pregnancy does not end happily.

LOVING CARE FOR
THE CHILD WHO DIES

Parents whose children die young should know that their child will continue to grow and develop in the astral realm. When a child dies, relatives or close friends who have died come and receive that child, and they nurture and care for it. In their sleep state, the parents also participate in the development of the child in the astral realm although they may have no waking recollection of this.

When the parents die, they are often taken to a center where they can view on a screen the development of their child to the present age, which could now be late youth or even middle age. This process is almost like a home movie, and it helps the parents to adjust from visualizing the child they remember to seeing and being reunited with the now-grown individual.

A SOUL'S CHOICE
MAY HAVE ADVERSE EFFECTS

Some people find it difficult to understand why two loving parents, who live godly lives, should have an offspring who, perhaps from birth, is negative and obstructive to all their values. I don't have all the answers. In some cases, however, the parents, when visiting the astral realm during sleep, may have made an agreement to provide a body for a specific soul to come into the world. At the time of birth, that soul may suddenly elect not to incarnate, or it may hold back a bit. Then, suddenly, a soul from the lower astral realms appears. Seeking in every way to come back to earth as quickly as possible, and without proper preparation in the heavenly realms, it may invade that waiting body and be a negative influence on that family.

On the other hand, in days like ours when abuse is a widespread problem in families, people ask why a soul would choose to come into a home where abuse of that child will occur. Again, I don't have all the answers, but I do know that a soul may have elected to come into a certain family, and then conditions can change. For instance, social and economic hardships may cause the parents to become abusive. The father may have lost his job. Becoming very distressed, he may then turn to drink. The mother may have lost her job. There may not be enough food, or heat, or clothing. Illness may strike, and the conditions become totally intolerable. The child may cry, perhaps just from hunger or illness, and the parents reach a breaking point that evokes abusive behavior.

Deprivation is so widespread in the world today. People have lost hope, and the disintegration of society is the result. This affects *everyone*. You cannot have a cancer in one segment of society and not have it spread throughout the whole. Healing must come for all if all are to benefit. Those who have much must put greed aside and share equitably with others. This is society's great task for the future.

THE DOORKEEPER

Heaven's net is indeed vast.
Though its meshes are wide, it misses nothing.

LAO TZU

ONE BEAUTIFUL SUNDAY morning in the early 1960s, A.D. and my brother, Al, and I attended services at New York City's Riverside Church. The Reverend Martin Luther King, Jr., was the guest preacher, and his powerful sermon on "Saint Paul's Letter to the United States of America" moved us profoundly. Inspired and excited, the three of us had a lively discussion about the service and Dr. King's message on our way back to my home in Westchester, where A.D. and Al were visiting us that weekend. I was deeply engrossed in our discussion as I drove north on the Henry Hudson Parkway. I was so caught up in it that as I turned into the Saw Mill River Parkway, I was completely unaware that fast traffic from the Bronx was merging in on my left.

Suddenly, I felt the steering wheel of my car being yanked by invisible hands. The car swerved sharply to the right—and in that split second, we avoided a shattering collision with a speeding car entering from that other highway. Had my steering wheel not been wrenched from my grip, we all could have been killed or very seriously injured.

A.D. has now identified my invisible protector as my "doorkeeper," and here he tells us about these invisible guardian/companions. The doorkeeper is not an angel but a human soul who accompanies an incarnating soul as far as the astral realm. He remains with the incarnating soul as a protector of the physical body throughout the entire incarnation of the soul. This is an important area of service in the realm beyond.

In addition to being our protector, the doorkeeper guards our privacy by "closing the blinds" on us when that is our desire. Even our loved ones who have died cannot intrude at such times. They can see what we are doing only when we are open to them and don't mind their observing us in that situation.

Our doorkeeper can guide us through thought, but he can never countermand our free will. We make his job difficult to impossible if we take drugs or have outbursts of violent rage. Both can tear the protective etheric web between our physical and spiritual bodies. Whatever the cause, such a renting of the web puts us in grave danger, and A.D. describes the perils we face and tells us how to avoid them as well as how to recover from them.

Every soul born is accompanied by a companion spirit that is dedicated to being that soul's helper from the astral realm throughout its incarnation. This companion is called a doorkeeper. The incarnating soul, in turn, may have been a doorkeeper for others at some time.

The doorkeeper descends with the in-coming soul only as far as the astral plane, and then remains very close to that soul for its entire lifetime. The primary function of the doorkeeper is to protect the physical body by preventing any astral entities from entering it when the soul vacates its body during sleep and ascends to the astral plane.

There are also instances when a doorkeeper has intervened, preventing physical disaster on the earth plane. People may wonder why physical disaster is not *always* prevented by a doorkeeper. I don't have an answer that would apply to all circumstances. I do know that people are always surrounded by God's love, but they need to exercise their free will and ask for protection. As the Bible says, "Ask and it shall be given." After they have asked, they then must be "open" to enable the heavenly helpers to assist them.

For instance, having sensed the potential for an accident on your usual route, your doorkeeper might try to influence you to think of taking an alternate route. If you are not open to this mental suggestion and don't follow it, then you could be involved in an accident. When you ask for protection and are spiritually open, the help is right there for you. If you haven't asked for protection, or if you are closed or "blocked," then the helpers either aren't aware of your need or they can't break through to you.

There are times, however, when averting physical tragedy may not be the ultimate goal for the incarnation of an individual. The soul comes into incarnation to grow. Though it has free will, it enters life with a matrix of situations that are to be experienced. The doorkeeper may try to protect an individual from anything outside of that matrix, but he can't interfere with situations that may be preordained. For instance, someone may suffer during an incarnation and accept that suffering in such a way that she or he demonstrates to others a great strength and faith in spite of the adversity. Not only does the soul itself grow spiritually by overcoming the adversity, but the example can inspire others and promote their spiritual growth. Actor Christopher Reeve, for example, is a person who, though paralyzed by a serious accident, is inspiring millions of people by the way he is coping with his disabilities.

Another duty of the doorkeeper is to protect the privacy of the incarnate soul. Even loved ones who have died cannot intrude on a person on earth unless the person reaches out for that connection. All people on earth are surrounded by a privacy that cannot be violated. We in the astral world are not allowed to see what is going on in a person's life unless that person calls on us to do so. I am not allowed to trespass in homes or intrude on people any more than I could do that when I was on earth. The privacy of people is respected.

When an accident causes sudden death, predeceased family and friends may not be aware that the person has died, so they won't be on hand for his or her arrival on the astral plane. The doorkeeper and other helpers assist the release from the physical body at the scene of death. They withdraw the astral body and accompany it to a center for healing and rehabilitation on the astral plane. This cushions the shock of sudden death. The doorkeeper then finds the newcomer's family and friends so that a reunion can take place.

The doorkeeper can guide through thought, but can never countermand the free will of the incarnate soul. When you sleep at night and are out on the astral plane, you meet your doorkeeper as an equal. When you die and again return to the astral planes to live, your doorkeeper may remain with you to help you adjust to living once again in the higher planes of existence. My companion and helper was a great blessing in helping me to adjust, and he is still with me. Your doorkeeper is dedicated to you until you don't need him anymore.

DRUG USE CAN HAMPER A DOORKEEPER'S PROTECTIVE EFFORTS

There are grave dangers in taking drugs. They do far more than damage the physical and astral body. You can see some of the drug users on earth sitting around in various states of hallucination. They have a pathetic look, as if they had no soul, and appear to be vacant behind the eyes. Many times they actually are vacant there. During a drug-induced trip they may actually be out of their body. Temporarily it is just a shell, sitting there and responding only to the physical mechanics of life. Often there are astral entities trying to get into that vacant body, and the drug user's doorkeeper has a terrible battle trying to keep those astral intruders from possessing it. This places the drug user in peril. There are times when one of those entities slips in, and then there is great trouble in removing that trespasser so that the owner of the physical body can come back.

Many other serious problems can result from the use of drugs. When we come into incarnation, the new personality we assume is protected by an etheric web between the physical and spiritual bodies. This enables us to function in a cohesive way, following the path our new personality is meant to take. Drugs, alcohol included, can damage that protective web, causing tears in it. Strong personality patterns from former incarnations can escape through those tears and seep into the current personality. This can be one of the causes of multiple-personality disorders and other mental illnesses.

Fits of rage or violence, drug induced or otherwise, can also tear the protective etheric web. It is unwise to give vent to violent anger, which is a searing and destroying force that can gravely damage both your physical and spiritual bodies. Anger produces a beet-red color in the aura, so when you encounter explosive anger either in yourself or others, concentrate on sending forth from within you a light that is white, blue, and gold. This will obliterate the red force and nullify its effect. Visualizing these counteracting spiritual colors will check any negative effects of anger within yourself. It will also act as a protective shield against anger directed at you by others.

Whenever there has been a tear in the etheric web, hope for healing can come through the power of prayer and psychic energy—if the injured person seeks healing and recovery.[11]

MEMORIES OF PAST LIVES

Life is the soul's nursery—its training place for the destinies of eternity.

THACKERAY

As OUR SOUL strives toward perfection, each of us probably has many sojourns on earth, living through many different incarnations. After meeting him several times at our meditation group, my friend Donna Piana, who was a mystic, identified A.D. as "a very, very old soul." Now that he is in the Beyond, A.D. has learned that this is true. At various sittings he has shared insights into a number of his previous incarnations. They range from being a philosopher of nature in the days of Aristotle to being a Catholic monk in medieval England. I've chosen three of them to present in some detail here, because they all contain significant evidential material in the way they impinged on his A.D. incarnation.

I have divided this chapter into three sections, one for each incarnation that A.D. describes, and I begin each section with a few observations of my own. During two of the sittings—the ones in which A.D. describes his life as a Buddhist monk and as a Jewish priest—Margaret received some extraordinary images from A.D. They moved her and me profoundly, and I have shared her descriptions with you in those sections, separating them from A.D.'s words by printing them in italics after the ornament that always begins and ends his remarks.

A BUDDHIST MONK

About a year after A.D. died, Margaret visited her family in Hong Kong. One day she and a few friends took a trip to a Buddhist temple on Lan Tau Island. While she was there, A.D. made a connection with her, and recalled being a Buddhist monk who had helped build that very temple.

Here, he describes the labor-intensive effort of building that temple, and he relates it to his efforts to gain justice for workers in his A.D. incarnation. This is certainly evidential material, because A.D. was Protestant chaplain of the Quad-City Federation of Labor in Illinois for more than eighteen years. He counted thousands of workers among his friends, and he often walked the picket lines with them when they were on strike.

In all the sittings we had, I had never seen Margaret break down and cry—until this one. She was quite overcome by the pictures of oppression she was being shown while A.D. was communicating to her. She was so upset that A.D. had to interrupt the session and leave for a while so that she could calm herself.

While Margaret regained her composure and we waited for A.D. to return, she described to me what she had been shown. That description is included between A.D.'s two messages at this session.

Here, A.D. begins by telling us how he discovered that he had been a Buddhist monk and what that incarnation taught him about the sacredness of work.

WHEN I FIRST came over here, I began to travel to various places on earth, but I felt no particular inclination to visit parts of the world that might connect me with the Buddhist religion. And then Margaret traveled to Hong Kong and took a side trip to the temple on Lan Tau Island. As she stood near the temple and gazed up the beautiful hillside, she was thinking, "This looks rather like the way A.D. described the invisible planes to me."

That did it. She connected with me. I came right in to see where she was—she "called" me there. As soon as I approached the area, I knew that I had been there before. I *knew* it. I *felt* it. The magnetic field of the place was immediately part of me. I stood and looked around for a long time. I wanted to see if I could recapture the *me* of that time. And I did. I was surprised to discover that I could begin to sense through that other, long-ago *me*.

I know now that when, as A.D., I preached a sermon, or got upset, or taught a class, I would sometimes be conscious that another facet of me was working. But I never really touched that part of me until that day on Lan Tau Island. I walked around. I looked at the rather sparse flowers, and I thought, "There were no flowers when I was here before. There was no paving back then, either."

I admired the paving stones and the atmosphere of the whole place. There were some rather shabby wood buildings, and I seemed to remember them. I managed to communicate to Margaret a desire to go back and ask her companion what all those buildings were a short distance away.

"That's where the nuns and monks live, and that is their refectory," her companion said. "We can all go and eat there. They'll open the doors about noon, and we can share their food, if we wish."

Well, they didn't wish. However, I did go and look at the long tables. I sat down at one, and I remembered that when I was there before, the building had only a roof and open sides, and we sat cross-legged on the earth. We didn't have any tables, and we didn't have any benches. Suddenly, I remembered that centuries-ago *me* very clearly. I was a most dedicated person, probably narrowly dedicated. All I thought about as that *me* was that the Lord Buddha had chosen me to help with my hands to build a resting place where he might be—a place where he might radiate his thoughts and his power, and where the people might come.

In the *me* that was before, I turned and looked, and I saw just a hillside. There were about eight or nine other men—some younger than I, some older, and some little boys—and I knew that we all had this one idea: to build a temple. I knew that we had no plans and I had no idea of how it was going to be built. However, we were all thankful to be here, where we felt that we were free and could be what we wanted to be.

It seemed to me that the first thing I had to do was to plant seeds and plants that we had brought with us through a lot of backbreaking effort. I looked around and said to one of the other men, "We need to plant these. We need to have food." I called some of the little boys, and we went across the way and started to clear the ground. It was easily cleared, and I could see myself planting. Then my thinking jumped over the years, and I realized that we had already reached the second tier of steps in our building effort.

Suddenly I came back to myself in the present, and I saw the finished temple. I saw the beautiful sweep of the roof. I saw the color of the doors, and I thought, "No. They weren't quite that color when I was here as that Buddhist." Then, instantly, I swung back again to me as that young Buddhist, putting color on those doors with a cloth. I didn't have a brush. I had a stick with a lot of cloth on the end of it, and I was applying a beautiful ocher-red color with that cloth. Then I came back to A.D., and I looked at the present color and thought, "It's not right."

A few seconds later, I heard Margaret say to her companion, "The paint's peeling off here. It looks like a different color underneath." And her companion said, "Yes, I think they've repainted it. It was more like a tomato color."

"Ah!" I thought. "I was right about the color I applied when I was here before."

THE SACREDNESS OF WORK

When I slipped back into that former personality, I couldn't quite recapture all the thoughts that had been in the head of that young monk. However, I could sense his dedication. I could capture the feeling of intense weariness, as if I was working to my capacity. I was very tired, and there were so many things to tend to. I was thinking in that personality, "What did I *achieve* in life?"

Suddenly the years rolled by very fast. I saw myself getting older and older. I saw myself as an old man, standing there talking to the people, telling them out of my own experience that labor is the offshoot of love. Through labor we can demonstrate our love. I realized that this is what I learned as that Buddhist, building that temple, and being in the aura of that situation: *The love of the Creator can be shown through work.*

I wonder now if maybe that is why I was always concerned with the worker in the incarnation of A.D. Was I concerned with the worker because I knew that *unless one gave love in one's work, the work was useless?* There were times, you know, when I could become emotional on the subject (and I'm making Margaret emotional now), but there were times when I could feel so full of the love of God that I could *burst.* And how can you express that love except through work? Work for yourself, and work for your family, and work for your fellowman. All of this is the expression of God.

How can we show people how wrong they are when they think that they can reach God through drug-induced hallucinations? Or through saying, "Oh, I can't take a job—I have 'spiritual' work to do. I can't clean a room—that's beneath me. I must *pay* someone to clean the room." I wonder how many people realize that the dignity of work brings us closer to the love of God. It makes my heart break sometimes to see such weakness, such stupidity. It also sometimes breaks my heart to see how people are striving and working for a pittance, and they are not told that God does not will this for them, but that they are working under these conditions because of man's inhumanity to man.

I will have to go for a minute, because I can't hold Margaret. She has become emotional.

***

Margaret had been moved to tears by the images she was given as A.D. communicated with her, and after he left, she put them on tape as she shared them with me. This is what she saw:

When A.D. was talking about labor, I saw peasants, and they were bent over and planting rice. It was very hot and very damp, and the women had their babies on their backs. They were being pushed and pushed. When it came time to eat, they barely had time to sit and eat a frugal meal, and then they were back again at their labor.

Then I saw little children in mines, pulling carts of coal—great, big carts—and they were falling down, and a cart ran over a little child's leg.

Then I saw women, and they were in a very hot place, washing what seemed to be masses of cloth. Sweat was running off them, and they were putting these long pieces of cloth over lines.

Another impression I received is that you can work hard out in the fields, doing things like felling timber or laying rails, and it doesn't seem so hard and so inhuman, because you're working outside. It seems much worse if you're working shut in and you're not seeing sunlight, or feeling the wind, or experiencing all of nature. The mere fact that you're outside, with nature around you, feeds into you, whether you know it or not. In the unhealthy conditions of being shut in, as in a mine, it's almost impossible to get to workers and help them.

Talking about what she had seen helped Margaret to get her emotions under control, and A.D. returned and continued his communication about his incarnation as a Buddhist monk.

***

I'm back again now that you're not so emotional. I'm not so emotional now, either. You see, I feel, looking back on my life as A.D., that I had to experience labor and work, and I had to be subject to the often heartrending experience of seeing other people in their work conditions. For I now realize that one of the most important missions of my work as A.D. was to bring the message that man must not degrade his fellows by subjecting them to conditions that don't even raise them out of the level of the animal.

Cruelty is latent in everybody. There are all the natural instincts in man, but all people should try to weed out cruel instincts as one weeds out harmful plants in one's garden. Just as we strive to grow a perfect rose in our garden, so we must strive to nurture and perfect the good within ourselves. We must also recognize and nurture that which is good in others.

No one can tell me that inhumanly sweated labor is to the glory of God. The people who are performing that type of labor are not the ones who are at fault. It is the ones who oversee and are aware of these inhuman conditions who are at fault. These conditions exist throughout the world today and must be rectified. People should never be sacrificed for profit. A fair profit is needed, but the welfare of people must not be sacrificed in producing that profit.

I want to add a little more about my experiencing of my Tibetan incarnation. When I went back into that environment and that personality, particularly as the older man, I discovered that I had been a Buddhist monk in a much earlier life too. In that first Buddhist incarnation, which was in China, I had pledged myself to come back and begin a new world on an island. And so, when I came back as that young man I saw on Lan Tau Island and started building that temple, I was fulfilling that pledge. Because I was a Buddhist monk for the second time, I was given access to all the knowledge that I had acquired formerly as the Buddhist monk in China who had studied all the philosophies of that period. I did not truly belong on any one ray, except a questing ray.

As A.D., I wasn't on any one ray, either. I was on all the octaves. I am told that after my Buddhist incarnation on Lan Tau, it was promised to me that from then on, I would not owe allegiance to only one path, but I would be a manifestation of the Whole. This has been revealed to me since I came here.

—◆—

A JEWISH PRIEST

In the days of the Old Testament, back when the children of Israel wandered the desert in the Babylonian Exile, A.D. experienced another incarnation as a clergyman. He has learned that he and Al served together in that time as Jewish priests, custodians of the Ark of the Covenant. Animal sacrifices were still performed, and A.D. tells us here of Al's reluctance to participate in them.

In their recent incarnations as A.D. and Al, they died giving their blood—A.D. in October 1970 of a ruptured vessel in his stomach, and Al in July 1971 of a ruptured aneurysm between his heart and spleen. A.D. has learned that this was to expiate their burden of those sacrificial killings. An interesting evidential sidelight to this account is that, as A.D., my father could never stand the sight of blood and was prone to faint when he saw someone bleeding.

When this sitting ended, Margaret described to me the images she had seen while A.D. looked back through time. As before, they are shared with you in italics after the ornament at the end of A.D.'s message, which now begins, and takes us back through the centuries to the wanderings of the children of Israel.

—◆—

I want to tell you about an incarnation I was shown, one that revealed to me that your brother, Al, and I were together as priests and custodians of the Ark of the Covenant in Old Testament times. As you know, the Old Testament and its account of the wanderings of the children of Israel in the wilderness always fascinated me. I'm now told it fascinated me because I was a priest at that time. It has also been explained to me that in my incarnation as A.D. I was also a priest, not just a pastor of a church, because the inner me was always worshiping. For as long as I can remember, I felt that way. I was always aware that if I just turned my thinking slightly, I would see the Light and the Glory of God. I knew I should be reflecting this Light, but there were times when the Light didn't come out from me as it might have.

There were also times, in that incarnation as a Jewish priest, when I forgot to radiate the Light. I fought and struggled and served the Lord my God by helping to bring my people out of captivity. I was serving Yahweh, the God that we understood at that time. We didn't understand then that God was all merciful, that God was all kind. We could not have understood it. Back then, we needed a God who said: "Now get on with it! You're being lazy—get moving!" Not one who would say, as Jesus said, "Come unto Me, all ye who are burdened and heavy-laden. Come to me, and I'll take your burdens and help you." No, we needed to hear, "You carry your own load and prove your mettle."

Do you see the difference? That was that period in the growth of man. It is true that we performed sacrifices. At that time it seemed the right thing to do. In other countries, even human sacrifices were being offered to other gods. It was a time when the spilling of blood was considered excusable under many conditions. If you didn't like someone— well, stab him in the back, get him out of your way. Unfortunately, people now do it another way, by stabbing on the psychological and mental levels, and that's just as evil in the eyes of the Lord God, because: "Thou shalt not interfere with thy neighbor."

We didn't interfere with our neighbors, but we took a lesser brethren, a lamb or a dove, to be our sacrifice. We believed back then that all life lives on all life, and all life sacrifices itself for all life. A man lays down his life for his friend. A lamb lays down its life for us, for the people as a tribe or nation. So the priest, acting as a mediator between the two, was quite sure that this was right.

I, in that incarnation, believed that too, and I wasn't afraid. However, the young priest who served with me—the person who came into my A.D. incarnation as my son—was always uncertain about animal sacrifice. He felt this letting of blood was not necessary. He was very tenderhearted. He came to be a priest more by accident. I was destined for the priesthood because I had been born into a priestly family, and from a small boy I had wanted to do what my father did. However, Al didn't. He really wanted to be involved in the music of worship, perhaps with the chanting of the cantor. For this reason, as far as I could, I spared him from participating in the sacrifices. Although he was not my son by blood in that incarnation, he was very much *like* my son, I being the older priest.

This was the reason why both Al and I died giving our blood in the past incarnation. It was a sacrifice to expiate the burden within us of those sacrificial killings. For me, it was no true sacrifice, because my work was finished. But for Al, it *was* a sacrifice, because his death has caused many people to seek the reason why a young man like that, full of promise, should die. Why should he leave his wife and children?

Deep within all of us is the awareness that there is a time to be born, and there is a time to die. The dying is sometimes much harder for the ones who are left than for those who come over. Al didn't find it as easy to come over as I did. He felt that he still had work to do. He is more inquisitive than I, now that he's here, but he's not prepared to talk too much about what he is doing. At present, he seems to be carrying on the investigations he began while on earth, and is seeking to learn more about communication between the Seen and the Unseen.

⬦

A.D. left us then, and Margaret told me about the images she had received as he communicated with her. Her words follow:

I saw the oddest thing then. I saw the globe, and I saw an ice cap. The ice was coming slowly down, and I began to feel as if we were freezing. Did you feel a drop of temperature toward the end?

I felt I was freezing, and I could see ice coming halfway down over England and quite a way down over Canada.

[She paused a moment as A.D. sent an explanation through to her.]

A.D. tells me now that he was showing me what the earth's condition was like when he was looking back into time. After the ice, I saw the most vivid picture of an oasis in the desert. The oasis was quite green and large, and there were many tents, just like the tents we see in the desert today, and people were living in them. There was the noise of goats and sheep. There were also donkeys and camels, and the ground was full of sheep. Dust was everywhere. A man dressed all in white was examining all the sheep and lambs. Then he would pick one up and take it with him. I suppose he was selecting it for sacrifice.

• • •

A RUSSIAN NOMAD

Back in the thirteenth century, somewhere around the time when the Inquisition was getting underway in Spain and Marco Polo was preparing to set off in the direction of China, A.D. experienced an incarnation as a nomad whose tribe wandered in the southern part of the country that is now Russia. He has learned that it was from this incarnation that he developed the interests he had as A.D. in agricultural labor and the plight of the migrant worker, and that it was also the origin of his fierce independence.

All this is certainly evidential. A.D. was appalled by the abominable working conditions of the migrant laborers who harvest our crops, and he fought to improve them throughout his life. Everyone who knew A.D. would also attest to his earnest independence. He was never afraid to stand alone to fight for a cause he believed was just, or to be a trailblazer in championing new ideas in the area of social justice. It may be that imprints from this former incarnation were also the reason for his keen interest in Russia when he was on earth. In the summer of 1938, just before World War II broke out, he made a special trip to Russia with a group of sociologists to study the conditions there. Much history intervened between that trip and the life A.D. describes to us here.

⊷⊰⊶

I have learned that I experienced a very significant life in Russia more than seven hundred years ago. I was able to review this life to link it into the interest I had as A.D. in agricultural labor and itinerant farm-workers. I didn't receive any thoughts or information about specific people living with me at that time. This review was given to me solely to show me the general conditions of that incarnation and why I developed such strong, ingrained feelings about easing the lives of migrant workers.

In that incarnation in what is present-day Russia, I was a member of a nomad tribe. We lived in the southern part of that vast country, and we had been in contact with warring tribes coming through from the Middle East. The land belonged to us as a tribe, and we worked together for the harvest. I was one of the planners for our tribe's sowing and reaping of crops. If we had a famine, we had to seek plants that grew in the wild. To survive, we frequently had to move on. Our life was a busy one, mostly centered on keeping hunger at bay in a stark environment. We were totally dependent on ourselves, and had neither organized charity nor a state. We alone determined our survival. That evoked a strong independence, which is a trait that I carried over into my incarnation as A.D.

Our religion centered on a benevolent God who gave rain, sun, and wind. We were much caught up in the cycles of nature. We prayed to and believed in a good God, but we were also aware of the evil in the world.

That life as a nomad, which was probably in a Mongolian body, left me with a sense of independence, a love of movement, a fondness for travel, a desire for freedom of thought, and a drive to always be on a quest for knowledge.

A REASSUMED PERSONALITY

Thus you will walk in the way of good men and keep to the paths of the righteous.

PROVERBS 2:20

IN 1972, ABOUT a year after he died, A.D. learned that there are times in the Beyond when a soul may reassume a past personality. He revealed this to us at a session that Margaret and I had invited a mutual friend, Jane, to attend. Jane's father, an immigrant from Germany, had committed suicide when she was fourteen, leaving her mother to care for her and her two sisters. Jane had always wondered why Margaret, who was able to see a Buddhist monk standing beside her as her guide, had never been able to contact her father, who had been a sensitive and caring man. That day, Jane hoped to get the answer from A.D.

The answer was surprising: The Buddhist monk Margaret always saw was actually Jane's father. That was why Margaret had never been able to contact the person Jane remembered. To help him grow and develop spiritually in the realm beyond, Jane's father had been allowed to reassume a former personality as a Buddhist monk.

After that session, I reflected on what A.D. had said to Jane, and it seemed to me that it might hold within it the explanation of an event in the Bible that has puzzled many of us. It is the account of the Transfiguration of Jesus on the mountain with Moses and Elijah, and the discussion that Jesus had with his disciples afterward:

> The disciples asked him, "Why then do the teachers of the law say that Elijah must come first?"
>
> Jesus replied, "To be sure, Elijah comes and will restore all things. But I tell you, Elijah has already come, and they did not recognize him, but have done to him everything they wished. In the same way the Son of Man is going to suffer at their hands." Then the disciples understood that he was talking to them about John the Baptist. —Matthew 17:10–13

This conversation takes place immediately after the Transfiguration, and it tells us that both Jesus and his disciples believed that John the Baptist was a reincarnation of Elijah. In that case, one might wonder why, since he was a reincarnation of Elijah, John the Baptist had not been the one to be there with Moses and Jesus on the mountain. After all, he, not Elijah, was the latest incarnation of that soul.

The information A.D. brought us in the session with Jane, which follows, may explain it. Perhaps John the Baptist had reassumed the Elijah personality in the realm beyond.

—◆—

JANE, YOUR DOORKEEPER tells me that your father had been deeply grieved over his suicide and its effects on your family. He was so remorseful that he had great difficulty adjusting to these spiritual realms. In addition, he was revolted by the terrible persecution he saw going on in Germany before World War II. He was profoundly distressed over this, and it made him ashamed of his German heritage. Further, he felt tainted by the awful things that were happening in Germany during the Holocaust. This added to his state of disfunction.

Your father had had a previous incarnation in Tibet as a famous Buddhist monk. With permission from the Lords of Karma, your father was allowed to reassume the personality from that former Tibetan incarnation. This enabled him to be in a more stable state, so that he could continue to grow and develop spiritually here. When he was that Buddhist monk, he had experienced a very productive life and great spiritual growth. The Buddhist monk that Margaret and other clairvoyants see beside you as a spiritual guide is actually your father in his former Tibetan personality.

Well, now I *myself* have learned something new today! That was something I didn't realize could happen, that sometimes a former personality could be reassumed. Jane, your father still feels very close to you, and even though he is now in that Tibetan personality, he wants to support and protect you in whatever way he can.

REINCARNATION
AND SEXUAL ORIENTATION

Anyone who claims to be in the light but hates his brother is still in the darkness. Whoever loves his brother lives in the light, and there is nothing in him to make him stumble.

1 JOHN 2:9–10

THOUGH HOMOSEXUALITY STILL meets with misunderstanding and even hostility in some segments of our society, we are living in a time when more and more homosexuals feel comfortable enough to be open about their sexual orientation. Some are able to discuss it in the public forum, and as they do, it becomes clear that many first experienced their sexual orientation at a very early age. These men and women say that homosexuality was not a matter of choice for them: they were born predisposed to it.

Biological factors could explain the origin of sexual orientation, and genetic studies of that theory are currently being conducted. Communications from A.D., though, have brought to light another possibility. For some men and women, he explains here, it is their imprint of past-life experiences on their soul that leads them into same-sex relationships.

———◆———

SOME SOULS COMING into incarnation as women still keep in the core of their being a desire for a close, loving, caring relationship with another woman. Their experiences in male/female relationships in other lives may have been hurtful and debasing, producing loneliness and a struggle to be respected as an individual. So now, instinctively fearing roughness and loneliness in this present life, they reach back to imprints of a past incarnation where they experienced happiness with an all-female group, maybe in a temple or a sisterhood, and they establish relationships with other women.

Likewise, some men, because of imprints of past incarnations and the customs of those times, come into incarnation and seek comfort, sustenance, and peace with another like-minded male.

Sexual attributes are but a small part of the feeling between the souls who are drawn together in this manner. The total pattern of their life is involved—the mental, the physical, and the spiritual. Often, the spiritual evolution of persons with this orientation can't progress unless the feeling of drawing together man with man and woman with woman is fulfilled. People who don't have these orientations find this difficult to understand. But when we consider that many patterns have evolved through the many lives of every individual, we can better understand the inclinations of some men to be with men, and of some women to feel more secure with women.

We need to concentrate on the "oneness" of all creation, and to understand that all human beings are God's people. We must seek to build a bond of unity among all persons, regardless of their past experiences or the particular path they must take toward a sense of wholeness.

SHARING GOD'S KINGDOM

I now understand that my welfare is only possible if I acknowledge my unity with all people of the world without exception.

Leo Tolstoy, *What I Believe*

WHEN HE WAS on earth, the Kingdom of God was the central theme of A.D.'s teaching. Throughout his communications from the Beyond, he has emphasized to us that God's Kingdom embraces *everyone*, and we are *all* an important part of that kingdom. In this communication he stresses that every human being must be treated with respect and dignity, regardless of condition in life, religion or lack of religion, and that the goal of all work should be helping one another and sharing with those who are less fortunate than we are. It is a message that those in the realms beyond evidently consider to be of primary importance, for A.D. noted before he left us that many souls had gathered to listen to him.

———◆———

WHEN I WAS a young man, I usually thought of God as a very stern Father. He was aware of what I did, and He wanted me always to get the best buy for my money. I got the reputation of being a very good shopper, and I'd tramp a long way in search of a bargain.

In the same way, we may now get the best from our efforts in life and work if we are aware of the fact that everything we have and do is for the glory of God. This is an old evangelical teaching, but, unfortunately, it was used by some early preachers in the wrong way. They would say, "Jesus was brought up in a poor home, and you are brought up in a poor home. You can know how Jesus lived. You have to be *thankful* you are poor. You should be grateful for the opportunities that come because you are poor." What nonsense!

So time has passed, and now we say, "There is equal opportunity for everybody!" Well, that is just not true. Due to prejudices that exist, there often is not equal opportunity for everybody. Also, not everybody is able to take advantage of the same opportunities. The human race is made up of individuals and every individual is different, so there must be inequalities—inequalities in money, inequalities in living conditions, inequalities in the kind of church we build, inequalities in the ways we can express ourselves. Some express themselves through art or music. Some through a garden, or through housework, or through making money.

There is nothing wrong in expressing oneself through making money, but it is what you do with what you earn from your work that is important. Money can generate tremendous energy for good. For example, you may be a compassionate person who is concerned about all the homelessness in the world. However, for various reasons, you may not be able to take a homeless person in to share your home. By giving money to shelters that serve homeless people, though, you can add to the energy of others working to alleviate the problem.

There is still a feeling of self-righteous superiority among so many people. A feeling that translates into, "I'm better than they are. Why should they expect to have what I have? Why should they expect to have a car, or two cars? I *worked* for it." Fine, you worked for it. But what do you do with the gains from your work? What do you do with your two cars? Do you hug them to your breast and say, "They're for *me!*"?

Or do you share them? How can we explain to people that what they have is part of God's Kingdom, and all of God's Kingdom is to be shared? It is only when we get a new insight through our soul's progress that we come to know this. Then we realize we must discipline ourselves.

What is discipline? It's a pruning. You can have a sweet-smelling lavender bush, but the lavender bush grows a very hairy, strong, tough, and rather dry stem. If you let it go without pruning, there will no longer be sweet lavender near the stem. It will only be out on the little far edges. Like the lavender, we must continually prune ourselves. We prune ourselves by prayer, and by meditation, and then we reshape ourselves and blossom in better ways.

When we come here to the Beyond and see ourselves, we can see where we have lopped and pruned, and we are able to go back in our thinking to what we were before the lopping and pruning. The sad thing is that sometimes we realize that we have lopped off something we should have kept. For instance, we should keep the fire of ambition, but we must remember to be ambitious for the whole of humanity and for the good of all. All personal ambition should be within a framework of consideration for other people. This applies to us as individuals *and* as members of a corporate structure.

I notice that a number of souls have gathered around me while I've been communicating with you. Evidently I'm speaking about something that is important to them: the dignity of work and the sacredness of each human being, regardless of station in life, or religion, or lack of religion.

FREE WILL
AND THE PROBLEM OF EVIL

Anyone who does wrong will be repaid for his wrong, and there is no favoritism.

COLOSSIANS 3:25

Down through the centuries, philosophers and theologians have been preoccupied by the Problem of Evil, and most of the rest of us have sought an answer to it too. If we and the world we exist in were formed by an all-good Creator, why do we find so much that is bad all around us and even within us?

When Margaret and I asked A.D. if he could shed some light on this enigma, he explained that our God-created universe is a perfect balance of positive and negative forces. Human beings, however, are endowed with free will, and its exercise introduces an interchange between the positive and negative aspects in us that can destabilize the balance of these forces.

Here, A.D. tells us the answers he has learned in the Beyond, and reminds us that the earth's natural resources are being depleted because of human greed. The environment was always a concern of his when he was on earth, and now he predicts grave consequences for our planet if we do not mend our ways. He also points out that we have produced a society with a throwaway mentality, and that this is being applied to people too. Human life is no longer valued and cherished, as it should be.

───────❖───────

Just as electricity has positive and negative states, and requires a balance of these forces to function, so, too, is the Universe composed of positive and negative forces. If it were all one, without the other to balance it, it would be frozen and unable to function. Miraculously, it is this opposition and yet perfect balance of forces that keeps the God-created Cosmos in being.

All creatures are created with this same polarity and are governed by this principle. Good, the positive, is the ideal force, but without the negative to balance it, there can be no growth.

Human beings, however, were endowed with free will, and that introduces freedom and choice, which lead to change. Change brings an interaction between our positive and negative aspects. As with electricity, a positive force meeting with a negative force results in a product that can be used for good or evil. It is the intent behind an action that makes it good or evil. The action itself is simply force.

The positive force is the spiritual energy within us, and when that is functioning, the negative force remains passive. However, if, through the exercise of our free will, we allow the negative force to take hold, it upsets the balance, creating sin or evil. Evil then becomes dominant and blocks the spiritual force from functioning. The German Holocaust of innocent Jews and other of God's children was an expression of the lowest in man. There the negative force was completely out of control, and we can say with certainty that this was the devil's work, the "devil" being the absolute negative force unleashed in the men who committed the terrible atrocities.

We, too, may encounter a negative obstruction in our thinking. We may try in devious ways to surmount the obstruction in our mind, but we will fail if we are not working in harmony with the Creative Law of

God. The secret that sets that law in motion is Faith active in Love. Hate, self-centeredness, avarice, and greed are powerful forces, and they are all aspects of sin or evil. So, too, is uncontrolled anger. If you allow it to take hold of you, it can damage your body and spirit. Such anger can be seen in your aura as a beet-red color. Visualize white, blue, and gold light to obliterate the angry red, and you will then feel a sense of calm and balance. Negative forces can be overcome and balanced only through the creative power of Love—love for the Creator and love for *all* fellow sojourners on the planet.

We must flow with the current of God, Who is the sustainer of life. If someone is going against this current and affecting you adversely, you must throw up a shield of protection against the negative and, with God's help, throw back positive aspects of behavior. By doing this, you can overcome evil with good and find harmony again.

I believe that there must be a settlement of accounts for all the negative things that are going on in the world today. It is unlikely that the world can go on without a great eruption. Unless we can change man's attitude and make him appreciate that his free will must be used for the good of all and not for personal gratification, the world will reap the consequences. Not until all souls have learned that lesson through their incarnations can we hope for true peace and prosperity. And that prosperity will not be defined in the terms you apply to it now. The depletion of its natural resources may compel the planet to revert to the way it was in the beginning. Picture only a few people populating the planet and everything being very calm and quiet—that may be what will come. The laws of God sustain all creation, and if we violate these laws, we reap the consequences.

WE HAVE NOT EVOLVED SPIRITUALLY

Today we are witnessing a turning in time's cosmic clock. Many of you are decrying—and I also would have decried—the selfishness of seeking to get away from responsibility, perhaps by retreating into self-centeredness, or smoking a reefer, or taking drugs to escape. If we could go back in time, we would find that such circumstances had occurred, but on a different level, when the caveman lived. Driven by hunger, he went out and killed an animal and brought it back to his cave. The animal was eaten, and then, because he wasn't hungry anymore, the caveman went into a stupor and didn't do another thing until he was hungry again.

The scenario these days is not much different: A youngster is hungry for an experience, and so he goes out and kills something—he kills a conventional idea by smoking a reefer or taking a drug. But our physical body and our spiritual body have become more sensitive over time. Because of this, that youngster's retreat from reality today has far deeper and more wide-reaching consequences than the caveman's lapse into laziness after killing and eating an animal.

Human beings are on a cycle of evolution. We have evolved physically and we have evolved scientifically, but we have not evolved spiritually. We've become slovenly in our thinking and have produced an excess of what we need. And now we can't distinguish our needs from mere desires. In earlier times, people hoarded because they were faced with scarcity. Later, when there was abundance, people cluttered their lives with objects and their minds with selfish thoughts. Man has gone to extremes and produced a society with a throwaway mentality. This has carried over to people, and now industrial society denigrates and throws people away as though they are worthless. Human life is no longer cherished and valued as priceless and precious, as it should be.

Man has made discoveries and developed inventions because God allowed him to. Knowledge and man's creations are not evil in themselves. It's the use to which we put them that determines their good or evil effect. People, through free will, often choose the wrong paths, and this is what allows evil to exist.

THE POWER
OF TRUE WORSHIP

"God is spirit, and his worshipers must worship in spirit and in truth."

JOHN 4:24

SAINT PAUL TELLS us that faith can move mountains. So, too, can the prayer it inspires, A.D. assures us here. Prayer is a powerful instrument for good in the world. When it is generated by group worship, it can be especially effective in helping to heal individuals and to mend nations torn by war. That is why it is important for us to pray together in our churches, synagogues, and mosques.

A.D. reminds us, however, that our responsibilities are not ended simply by gathering together and praying jointly in our houses of worship. It is equally important for us to realize that God's house is within each of us: *we* are the temple of the living soul. Religion can help us to attain wholeness of being, but true worship is more than religious ritual. True worship is manifested in the way we live our life.

It is not what creed we profess, but rather it is our own inner quality of life that determines whether we will be in "Heaven" or in "Hell" when we pass on to the spiritual realms.

———◆———

WHEN PEOPLE GATHER together in a group, singing and praying as one, their true worship generates light that can combat the darkness in the world. This is one of the reasons why, even if you don't agree with every ritual performed in a church, or temple, or mosque, you should go to God's house and participate in worship there. The energy for good that you will leave behind is as important as the renewal and strength that you will take away at the end of the service. Not only will this positive energy, which is produced by group prayer, sustain your minister, your choir, and your congregation, but it will also be a source of help to those who are absent. It may even sustain some who know nothing at all about the value of prayer.

We from the spiritual realm join you in your houses of worship, and your power and our power mingle as you pray, generating a mighty energy that can be used for healing individuals and counteracting the upheavals within nations. This energy can be seen by a clairvoyant as a powerful light, and its rays can reach out and touch the lives of those in need.

There are those from here who go to prepare the atmosphere of the house of God before you arrive. They "sweep" the atmosphere clean, almost like anointing the sanctuary. If you always sit in the same pew, there is an auric egg there ready for you to settle into. That is why when you go to worship, you fidget if you're not quite in the place where you usually sit. You like to sit in your usual place, because then you feel comfortable and at home.

Now, all this was news to me. It's something I sensed when I was on earth, because, when I was teaching, I disliked my students to sit in different places. I'd say, "Come on, you were sitting here last week, come back. I've gotten used to your being there." I thought it was *me*. In my ignorance, I didn't realize that it is this auric pattern—this light, this form, this substance—that we can see from here, which is there for you to fit into. When a stranger arrives at a place of worship, he goes through a process of getting used to it, settling down, being received, and feeling warmth generated. He makes a place for himself where eventually he, too, will feel comfortable and at home.

The founders of our religions gave us hymns to help us release our energies as we lift ourselves in song. They gave us words and liturgy to release our cares. They advocated silence so that we may become aware, and preaching so that we may listen. These elements combine to produce exactly the right balance in us. It is unfortunate that some people enter a house of worship only to give lip service. Let's hope that they receive something in spite of themselves. We need to observe a day of worship. When we ignore or remove the Lord's Day, we're playing into Satan's hands. But please don't think of Satan as a Being. It's a Force.

Though it is important to gather together in our houses of worship, we must also realize that God's house is within each of us. We are the temple of the living soul. We need to be mindful of this not only on our days of worship but also on every day of the week. Therefore, we should look after our bodies more than we do. We should eat a proper diet, and we should exercise our body more, because it is God's temple, the dwelling place of the soul.

CHURCHES SHOULD NOT ISOLATE PEOPLE

I want to say something about the divisions among the churches. When we talk about a church, we think about the group of people who go to that particular church—and my church may not want to have anything to do with your church, or his or hers, and so we're isolated from one another. This may have been suitable in the past, but it is not suitable for the present or the future. It is more important to be aware of all the other people on earth and to know that you are all inhabiting the same space, traveling the same road, sharing the same period of time, and that you are all children of God. That can be an overwhelming revelation. When somebody on earth sits in his car at a traffic light and looks across at the next person and thinks, "Goodness, he, like me, is a child of God," that can be a more truly religious experience than any religious ritual. It is this kind of awareness that will eventually break down barriers between religious groups.

TRUE WORSHIP IS LIVING YOUR LIFE IN CONSTANT COMMUNION WITH THE GOD OF LOVE

From here when I look at a flower, I see not only the pinkness of its petals and the gold of its center but I also see the picture made by its perfume—delicate whirls of fragrance emanating from it. I may not understand the perfume that I see, but do I need to understand it in order to give grateful thanks for it? Isn't it enough just to be aware of this precious gift from God?

And so it should be through all Creation. We say, "Thank you for what we are about to receive. Thank you for what we have received." What do we mean when we say "thank you"? Are we saying it in deep gratitude? Or are we saying it simply because it's very nice to have certain things? Is our "thank you" the equivalent of, "Yes, I will have another cup of tea"? Or is it an acknowledgment that we recognize that all things belong to God and are part of God?

Throughout the world today, religions are spreading. I say religions in its plural construction because I am surprised when I travel around the world and see the many, many thousands who belong to no formally recognized house of worship, and are just gathering together or thinking. And there are also a great number of people who pray without ceasing. They reach out and sense God through the quietness, the calmness, the oneness that comes perhaps from watching a bird, or sending out a thought, or looking at a cloud in the sky. For those people it is hardly necessary for us to say more than, "You're right, my friend. You are part of God. You are part of the Heavens. You are part of the Astral World and part of the Spiritual World. You are part of each, and you belong to God." A person's religious label is not important. It is the spiritual quality of his or her life that matters.

The spiritual laws of behavior and being are the same for everyone. It makes no difference whether you go or don't go to a church, temple, or mosque. It is your quality of life that will determine your being in "Heaven" or "Hell" when you come to the spiritual realms. Religion can help you attain wholeness of being, but some who profess to be an agnostic or an atheist may actually express God's Spirit within themselves better than many people who have professed a religious creed but are narrow in their views. By their actions, some agnostics and atheists actually demonstrate a more Godly quality of life.

When on earth, I had a friend who insisted that he didn't really believe in God. I told him I thought that very strange, and asked him if he wasn't the one who was always concerned about the welfare of others and was always the first to help someone in need. He agreed that perhaps this was true. I then told him I believed that these good works were actually evidence of God working in and through him. "Well, I'll be damned!" he said, astonished.

God often works anonymously through people. When they have lived exemplary lives in tune with God's laws of love, God gathers these children to Himself on their arrival here. They then know the Power that had been motivating them.

True worship is more than religious ritual—it is how you live your life. When Saint Paul said, "Pray without ceasing," he meant, "Live your life in constant communion with the God of Love."

WAR'S DESTRUCTIVE EFFECT
ON THE WORLD BEYOND

They will beat their swords into plowshares and their spears into pruning hooks. Nation will not take up sword against nation, nor will they train for war anymore...for the Lord Almighty has spoken.

MICAH 4:3–4

IN DEATH AS in life, A.D. has shown great concern about the social problems that prevail around the world, and he has been deeply distressed over the turmoil he is witnessing from the Beyond. Throughout our communications with him, he has anguished over the inhumanity that is rampant, from the starvation in Somalia to the massacres in Cambodia and Rwanda, the bloodletting in Liberia, and the turmoil in the Middle East. In May 1995, when Margaret was visiting me in Maine, A.D. spoke to us about his great distress over the Bosnian War. He had been working with a group from the Beyond assisting the dying in Bosnia, and he was shaken by the horror all around him.

The distress that comes through in A.D.'s messages is consistent with the torment he felt over the horrors of war when he was on earth, which was almost more than he could bear. When the atomic bombs were dropped on Japan in August 1945, he was so distraught that he told us that were it not for his faith in God, he would have drowned himself in the ocean. It was his knowledge that God was still in charge, he said, that gave him the strength to maintain a sense of wholeness and balance, in spite of his devastating sorrow over the atrocities of the war and the bombing.

In the message that follows, A.D. describes the turmoil created in the realms beyond by the chaos in Bosnia. The torment he still feels over the ravages of war and the violence and cruelty that the peoples of earth inflict upon one another is apparent. He tells us that we on earth who are appalled by the eruptions of violence and cruelty must join together and use the power of prayer to exert a healing force and positive energy to overcome the evil. He also issues a warning to those people who conduct wars and commit violence in the name of religion: Their acts are abominable in the sight of God; they are not acting under His instruction or protection. Those who believe that they will be rewarded in heaven for killing others on earth will discover that they have instead a long and onerous karmic debt to pay.

⟶⟨⟩⟵

The Bosnian situation has caused great turmoil here in the Beyond. The huge influx of disturbed astral men, women, and children who are victims of that war has brought with it grave concern and great pain. We have to learn to be as objective as possible as we work with these souls. Otherwise, the deep compassion we feel for them can lead to our taking on the yoke of their suffering. Then our despair over the evil conditions that brought them here could cause a terrible disintegration within us.

As I work with these souls, I need to draw on my faith as a Christian, on my knowledge that God Himself takes on the yoke of that suffering for us. I remind myself that He demonstrated this through the death of Christ on the Cross, and that God *did* and *will* overcome evil. We ourselves don't have to take on this burden, which is too much for us to bear. Our task is to center ourselves in our loving Creator, and, acting as His servants, to serve with love and compassion those who suffer. We, too, may suffer as we carry out our task, but if we are centered in God's Love, we can bear that suffering without any sense of personal disintegration.

The Killing Fields are everywhere. Rage and anger, fear and agony, hate and desire to destroy have become common feelings that assail the senses, causing wounding and death around the globe. As hard as we who work for the Lord try, we seem unable to put an end to this hatred. I assure you that those who fight for liberation from oppression are under the protection of the Love of the Lord. When you think of them, visualize the Gold Light to protect them. Pray with me for them.

Hate is a powerful vibration. We try to overcome it from the Beyond by projecting love and compassion in an effort to bring quietness and peace. Your human efforts can't succeed unless you band together, amassing your healing forces to overcome the destructiveness of hate. The Light *will* prevail, but not until a new approach comes with great force. The Sword of Righteousness is unsheathed for this battle, but how can the ordinary man, woman, or child fight unless in the armor of God? This must be our effort—to put on the whole armor of God. Here, I meet with others of like mind, and we link together using God's Love Power. We are buffeted by all the negative forces emanating from earth: rage, anger, hatred, revenge. We need the Breastplate of Righteousness to protect us from the onslaught of evil.

I have joined an army of helpers here, dedicated to releasing souls trapped inside mangled bodies in Bosnia. Heaps of corpses lie around, empty of their former inhabitants. From afar we see clouds of flashing colors, flickering lights, dark patches. Sounds of all kinds surround us. When we work in these areas, we are clothed in gold, like a suit of armor. Under the direction of spiritual and etheric forces, we try to embrace and lift up those we can reach, helping them into peaceful areas. This resembles the work carried out by ambulance attendants, nurses, doctors, and clergy after a battle on the physical plane. It is amazing, the number of souls from here who answer the call to work in this way. This work is carried out wherever there is war and conflict. It is an unending task.

I can tell you that it is easier for you on earth to remove the dead physical bodies than it is for us to assist in releasing the souls of those bodies. A normal death, as you know, is attended by the dying person's helpers and by the souls of deceased relatives and friends. Death then becomes a very orderly and, usually, loving and caring event. The body is left in quietness, and the soul in its astral, colorful, etheric covering is guided away from it lovingly. But death on any battlefield where there is hatred, fear, anger, and anguish of mind, as well as physical pain, is a chaotic experience. Very few deaths in such circumstances are free from the anguish and fear evoked by the terror of war, with its blasts of battle and screams of shells and people. Certainly those who have died earlier come to help their loved ones on these battlefields, but even those loved ones find it difficult to make the soul's transition easy.

Once the released souls are removed to an area of peace and quiet, they are greeted by waves of Love. Harmonious waves of pity and compassion encircle them and heal them. Love breaks the bonds of fear, and it eases pain from physical and mental wounds. From the high reaches of Love gentle dews of calm and peace rain down. Hold fast to this: Good *can* overcome Evil, but *love must replace hate.* Please practice that in your own lives. It is extremely important.

You may tend to despair, asking yourself, "What can *I* do?" My answer is, "You can pray." Your individual prayers are important. One small candle for peace and light is *very* important, because that beam goes out and joins with those sent out by others who are also praying for peace and light. The combined power achieved through group prayer is even more helpful, so it is also important for you to gather together in prayer and meditation groups and send the power of Love to the areas of the world where it is needed. There *is* force in prayer, and there is healing in that force when it is generated by Love. Your prayer power on earth then joins with our prayer power here, and the energy of Love that they combine to create is a great force for Good in overcoming Evil.

Men who conduct wars in the name of religion are not doing so under God's aegis, and those responsible will have great spiritual reparations to pay. The damage done by war to individuals and societies is counter to all the laws of peace and love that God has given mankind to follow. Love, God's energizing force, is the only way to achieve the ultimate state desired for all humanity. Love is a force for achieving integration and wholeness. Hatred and violence achieve only disintegration and destruction.

Those who believe they will be rewarded in heaven by killing others on earth will have an enormous karmic debt to pay. Remember, you bring to the spiritual realms your own state of being, and that is your heaven or your hell. Religious zealots who believe that they will be rewarded in heaven for killing others on earth are rewarded only by being condemned to the Realm of Darkness. There, with all other believers that war and conflict are the only way to solve problems, they are doomed to continue their destructive behavior. This can drag on for eons. During that time they are confined to their battlefields and experience continuously the hell of war. There is no relief for them until they begin, one by one, to realize that they are accomplishing nothing. When that realization occurs, they can begin to be drawn out toward the Light. Then begins a process of rehabilitation and growth toward fullness of life in a context of love and concern for others. This process takes far longer in the spiritual realms than in the physical realms. Therefore, people who adhere to violence and cruelty should change their thinking and behavior and turn their efforts toward peace while they are still incarnate on earth.

When people who were drafted against their will to participate in war arrive here, they don't carry a heavy karmic debt. They are released into the Realms of Light and immediately begin a period of healing and rehabilitation to help them overcome any burden of guilt created by their participation in war's destructive force. This also applies to those who participate in a strictly defensive war, a war not of their own choosing, or in an international peacekeeping force.

As long as there is evil in the world there will be a need for police actions using force to contain it, both on a national and international level. The ultimate goal, however, should be to eventually attain a state of cooperation and love among all people, thus eliminating any excuse for conflict and the need to contain it.

The Earth is a planet for learning. Yet for centuries mankind has turned it into a planet of wars. Why is it that humanity has never learned the futility of war in achieving God's purposes for us on Earth? Pray that individuals and nations may gain new insight and come to know that war is not the answer.

THE POWER OF LOVE
AND PASSIVE RESISTANCE

Nonviolence is the first article of my faith. It is also the last article of my creed.

GANDHI

ONE OF A.D.'S FAVORITE BIBLE TEXTS was Matthew 5:43–44, the saying of Jesus: "You have heard that it was said, 'Love your neighbor and hate your enemy.' But I tell you: Love your enemies and pray for those who persecute you."

As a minister, A.D. preached this gospel of love and reconciliation, and as a man, he lived by it. He believed strongly in the power of passive resistance to overcome evil in the world and change it for good. Now, from the Beyond, he continues to bring us the message that Love is the true force for change in our world. Here, he confirms it as he tells us of some of the martyrs who have proved it by their example and sometimes with their lives, and who find the heavenly reward of true peace.

———◆———

GREAT POWER FOR GOOD has come through passive resistance and demonstrating love for one's enemies. Jesus, asking God's forgiveness for those who were crucifying him, is the foremost example for Christians, and certainly a great influence for many non-Christians as well. Jesus made such an impact on human history that the calendar of Western Civilization makes his life the central reference point. Events that occurred before his birth are referred to as happening B.C.; those that occurred after it are dated A.D.

Following in the footsteps of Jesus, Martin Luther King, Jr., preached nonviolence while leading the struggle for civil rights and equality for black Americans. Although he was assassinated by his enemies, his life became a cornerstone for the continuing struggle for justice and equality for all people. Also a Christian, Nelson Mandela advocated nonviolence while leading the black people of South Africa in their long, painful pursuit of justice and equality in that nation. Although he was imprisoned by his enemies for decades, he became a rallying point in his country, and inspired the breakdown of its oppressive apartheid system.

While demonstrating the way of passive resistance to win independence for India, Mahatma Gandhi, the great Hindu leader, was imprisoned many times and was eventually assassinated by his enemies. Gandhi is still revered throughout the world as the great soul who, through personal sacrifice, forced the British government to grant his nation independence.

Exiled from his Tibetan homeland by the Chinese, the Dalai Lama preaches and personifies for Buddhists, and for the whole world, the principle of nonviolence and reconciling love toward all people. President Anwar el-Sadat of Egypt was assassinated in his homeland when he, a Muslim, stood firm for reconciliation and peace with Israel. And Prime Minister Yitzhak Rabin, a Jew, was assassinated in Israel for promoting peace with the Muslim world.

Through their martyrdom, whether through death or exile, these souls have pointed the Way for mankind to evolve to greater spiritual dimensions. Losing one's physical life is not to be feared, for great spiritual progress is often made through that sacrifice. Martyrs like these come to our heavenly realms with a sense of integration and wholeness within themselves that is a source of great contentment and peace, because they have been instruments to point the Way of reconciliation and Love for all of mankind.

The darkness can be overcome, but the change must come within the heart and mind of each and every human soul. That is the task before us.

A JOURNEY THROUGH
OUTER SPACE

When I consider your heavens, the work of your fingers,
the moon and the stars, which you have set in place,
what is man that you are mindful of him,
the son of man that you dost care for him?

PSALMS 8:3–4

In the fall of 1976, A.D. asked Margaret to begin to train me so that I, too, could be a direct receiver for him. Margaret immediately began working with me, and by the time she returned to England, we were having good results. Since then I have continued to take dictation from A.D. on an occasional basis. I don't claim to be a receiver to the extent that Margaret is, nor do I aspire to that, but I have found these contacts with my father to be very rewarding and nurturing.

When Margaret was visiting me in May 1995, she came down to breakfast one morning and was obviously upset. She said she was told during the night that A.D. planned to leave us. She had the impression that this would be like a "death" in the Beyond, that he'd be going into a far plane, never to return. Later, A.D. assured us that this wasn't the case. He had been given permission to go on a scientific mission with a group of souls interested in exploring the far reaches of outer space. It would be necessary for those who went on this mission to assume an entirely different body form in order to enter the higher dimensions, but he would be able to return to the spiritual dimensions connected with Earth and again be clothed in the form necessary to function near us. The expedition would begin at the end of May, and the participants would probably return sometime in late December.

When we asked A.D. why he wanted to go on this journey, he said that he had developed a "scientific bent" during an incarnation as a natural philosopher in the days of Aristotle. The scientific component of his inner self had come to the forefront, and his desire for knowledge in this field had led him to seek permission to join the expedition.

The reference to his "scientific bent" is evidential. While on earth, A.D. was extremely interested in science, especially astronomy and geology. There were excellent departments in both at Augustana College, which was connected with the seminary where he taught for over thirty-six years. I have treasured memories of the times he took my brother and me down to view the heavens through the telescopes at the college observatory. And he often arranged for his students to attend special lectures at the geology department of the college, so that they could acquire a background on evolution for interpreting the biblical accounts of creation.

A.D. trained for this space expedition for a long time with other souls who had previously made such explorations. In a communication from my husband, Hal, I learned that my mother didn't want A.D. to make the trip, and that A.D. himself was a bit apprehensive. In the end, his eagerness to know, and his dedication to the group he had trained with, overcame his anxieties, and so he went as planned.

On his return in January 1996, A.D. elected to use me instead of Margaret as the receiver of information about his fascinating experiences in outer space. Margaret told me this was because she and her late husband, Edward, were avid readers of science fiction, and were also very interested in astrology. A.D. was afraid that this background might cloud her receiving information about his journey from him, leading her to question whether some of it sprang from her subconscious mind. I, on the other hand, had little interest in science fiction, astrology, or even astronomy. Therefore, I would be a clear channel.

As I write this, our scientists' quest for evidence of life on other planets is expanding at a dizzying rate. Early in 1997, they were debating whether an ancient meteorite might actually have come from Mars and bear signs of early life on that planet. That spring, the spacecraft Galileo beamed back photographs of Jupiter's moon Europa, and scientists saw a great possibility of a global ocean beneath its surface, an ocean that could be the cradle of extraterrestrial life. And in the summer the spacecraft Pathfinder landed on Mars and began transmitting pictures of that planet and exploring its dusty surface for signs of life.

Scientists and engineers continue to try to build spacecraft that will take astronauts farther and farther from our own atmosphere. Yet, what I learned from A.D. makes me wonder about the efficacy of their efforts to extend manned space exploration. For, as A.D. tells us in the report that follows, even in his after-death state of being, he had to be protected from the conditions of outer space by changing his body form and substance.

<hr />

WELL, RUTH, I'M back, and I experienced no adverse effects from the trip. Our body form had to be changed to enter the other dimensions, but through the power of thought and with the help of the Lords of Form, we have been able to recover the body form we had before we left. The central core of our being—our soul, or seed atom—was unchanged throughout the entire process.

I'm going to tell you my personal experiences and impressions of this journey. I can't give you a scientific textbook on the outer reaches of God's domain, since much of our experience involved the higher dimensions of existence and it would be difficult to translate this into terms you could understand. I do, however, want to share the tremendous spiritual implications of our journey. It is this message that's important. I want people to know that they are each an important part of a universe so vast that it defies comprehension.

There were twenty-two of us in our group, and we went out to the other realms in a balloon-shaped vehicle. Our bodies were very slender, almost sticklike in form, and our eyes were considerably larger and looked something like goggles. It was almost like donning a Halloween costume, but it was necessary for protection in the dimensions we were entering. I can't explain the content of our body form, which was entirely different from the substances needed near Earth. I can only describe our appearance. Within that strange-looking shape, our soul essence—our driving and motivating force—remained unchanged. While on our mission, we had no sense of body weight. We were aware of a cohesive self, but were completely weightless.

There is no time or space where we are, so it is difficult to describe the sense of vastness we experienced. Many planets and stars surrounded us at all times, and we were literally transformed in our comprehension of reality. The universe is far more expansive than I am yet able to fathom. I marvel at the *mind*—the Creator behind it all.

We found no life on Mars, and that was a disappointing discovery, since we had thought there would be life on that planet. However, there are inhabitants on many millions of planets, and some are very different from us on Earth. Wherever we went, we encountered no hostility. The way had been prepared for us by our "tour guides." All of these areas are under the one creative force that we call God, and we could sense this cohesiveness. This took away any fear of the unknown that we might otherwise have had.

There are social bonds among the peoples we contacted, just as there are on Earth. There is also evidence of some moral struggle and evolvement among these inhabitants. We learned that we can, with permission, make a decision to incarnate on another planet in another galaxy, if we wish. Some do. However, each planet was populated by the Creator in its own unique way. A permanent change of form would be necessary to shift to living in another environment. We found that illness strikes other body forms, just as it does the human form. There were hospitals or healing centers wherever we found an inhabited planet, so there is no "perfect" body form that does not have a few problems now and then.

Venus was one of our stops, and we found people there more closely resembling Earth people than on the planets in the outer reaches. Being closer to Earth, the inhabitants function in a manner similar to that of Earth.

Wherever we visited, we found much interest in interplanetary exploration among the inhabitants. The UFO's often reported on Earth are real. They do exist, and they were active millennia ago. They were reported in biblical writings: Elijah and others were "ascended."

The power UFO's use and generate is even greater than nuclear power, and it's beyond our current understanding. UFO's also have a feature that enables them to "tune in" to the density of Earth's properties. When they enter Earth's atmosphere, they assume the solidity of Earth density and "appear" to inhabitants of the planet. They can later shed this density and reenter the dimension that is natural to them. They then appear to vanish from the sight of Earth people who have seen them. This dimension funnels down through all of the Earth planes, and back up again.

It is difficult to describe the multidimensional reality that exists beyond your three-dimensional realm. It is all rather mind-boggling. Though I have experienced these outer planes, I'm still not able to explain them in any way that you would understand. Perhaps it is enough to say that the whole Creation is incredible. There is but *one* Lord and Sustainer of the Universe. Monotheism is correct, but the manifestations of God are incomprehensible.

I wanted to be part of this expedition so that I could experience the great reaches of the universe and thus have a greater knowledge of the tremendous dominion of our Creator God. I learned more than I had hoped for.

Galaxies are not even the ultimate pattern. Creation is infinite, and infinite means just that—*infinite*. Finite mind simply cannot comprehend the extent of all aspects of creation. Our knowledge can be only fragmentary. But now, more and more, within the depths of my being, I know reality's essence. Utter amazement prevails when I try to reflect on this knowledge. That I am part of this great creation, and a "son" of the Most High, gives me a sense of overwhelming peace and contentment. Now I am prepared for anything that may come to me in the future.

I'm glad I made the journey, but I feel that Earth and its atmosphere are my true home. We are working here for the Lord and His work on Earth, and we need links to persons in the physical dimension on that planet as partners in the process. The Earth is the Lord's and the fullness thereof—all they that dwell therein. The Earth *is* important, *very* important, to God the Creator. He sent His Son, and He was incarnate in that Son to identify with the Earth, which He loves. The Earth is so important to Him that not a single atom of it is without His concern or blessing.

Evil and sin are rampant on Earth, and spiritual evolution will not take place unless we can convince people that they themselves are a very important part of this vast, great, magnificent Whole. A new theological concept is going to emerge in the coming age. This new theological approach will see a merging of many faiths, all seeking *one truth:* The God of Love is the God of *all*, and He will overcome.

We were around you at Christmas, helping you celebrate the birth of Jesus. I now have a better understanding of the meaning of his birth and life. It relates to a far greater Whole than any of us realized when I was on Earth. Jesus is a true manifestation of God the Father, but God the Father reaches eternally through universe after universe. The fact that God has related to man in such a personal way as through the person of Jesus Christ is a miracle in itself. We now know that this same *potential* of Godlike being has been given to the soul of each and every man, woman, and child who is born, regardless of race, creed, or color. We must always try to be God-centered, for that is the expression of our true selves. This "centering" continues as the most important process of existence, even after we have passed from your life to ours.

PART FOUR

THE JOURNEY
CONTINUES

LOVE'S TOUCH FROM BEYOND

*They that love beyond the world cannot be separated by it.
Death is but crossing the world, as friends do the seas; they
live in one another still.*

WILLIAM PENN

ABOUT SEVEN MONTHS after A.D. died, my brother, Al, and I drove to
Ten Mile Lake in Minnesota, where A.D.'s cabin was located. That
cabin had meant a lot to A.D. It was his retirement home, his little corner of contentment in our worrisome world. Al and I and our families
had had many happy times with him there, but it was too far away from
our homes for either of us to turn it into a weekend retreat.
Reluctantly we decided to sell it. We went there that weekend to sort
through the contents, clean it up, and make it ready for sale.

Although it was May, the ground was still covered with snow in the
north country, and the sturdy log cabin was a cozy place to be. The man
who took care of the cabin for us had come in earlier to air it out and
turn on the water and the furnace, so it was cheerful and welcoming
when we arrived.

We put on our old cleaning clothes, and I sorted and vacuumed and
dusted upstairs while Al concentrated on cleaning the basement. There
was a lot to be done, and we worked hard at our various tasks all day.

We had brought food with us, but at dinnertime Al suggested that we take a break, put on some respectable clothes, and eat at a restaurant across the lake.

We changed, locked up the cabin, and drove around the lake to the restaurant. It had begun to snow, and we felt warm and cozy, watching the snowflakes float to the ground outside as we ate and reminisced. It was a lovely dinner, a special brother-sister time of shared thoughts and memories, and I shall treasure it always. Neither of us could have known, but it was to be one of our last times together. Only six weeks later Al died unexpectedly of a ruptured aneurysm.

After dinner, we went back to the cabin, put on our old clothes, and returned to our chores. I went to the kitchen to fill my scrub pail with water, but none came through the tap. Puzzled, I went into the bathroom and tried to draw water there. Again, no water.

I called to Al in the basement and told him of the problem. He went over to the water intake valve and found that it had been turned to the off position. Startled, he called me to come down to the basement to see it. We stood there together gazing at the turned-off valve. The water had been on full force all day. We had locked the cabin when we left, and no one had been in other than ourselves. Filled with a comforting sense of wonder, we both felt our parents' presence. We were certain that they had turned off the water as a signal that they were indeed there with us.

The next time Margaret was with me and we were having a sitting with A.D., he confirmed our conclusion. "We wanted you to know we were there," he said. "It takes a lot of power and effort to do this, but the conditions were right and we were able to make it happen."

What Al and I witnessed in A.D.'s cabin that long-ago evening is called a telekinetic manifestation. It is a physical event that defies explanation in terms of physical causation. It can be accounted for only as having originated from psychic causation. Simply put, it is the movement of an object caused by the mind of a distant and unseen human, living or dead.

Dr. J. B. Rhine, the world-famous parapsychologist from Duke University, conducted many studies in the field of telekinesis. In his book *New World of the Mind*, he reports on his findings and makes this observation about manifestations that could be caused by deceased persons:

> Many of the physical effects reported are associated with death. The clock stops, a picture falls, a window shade flies up, or a vase breaks, all in some unexplainable fashion at the time a person connected with the object dies.... Even when the event is not associated with the moment of death, it often may be attributed to the agency of a deceased individual.... It would be scientifically unthinkable to consider any of these reports of spontaneous occurrences as acceptable proof of anything. It is quite enough to take them as things that people say happen to them; and when enough people say the same kind of thing, no matter how strange and incredible it may be, it is wise to look into the facts, letting the interpretation wait. There are always perfectly *safe* ways of looking into such matters. Such looking and the follow-up researches make up the advances of science.[12]

In the years that have passed since Al and I stood side-by-side before that water valve I have experienced several other telekinetic happenings. One, which I admit could be explained away, happened when I flew from Portland to Washington to spend Christmas 1995 with my son and his family. Knowing that A.D. would soon be reporting his experiences in outer space to me because I would be a clearer channel than Margaret, I thought I should learn a little more about the subject. With this in mind, I purchased a paperback copy of Carl Sagan's book *Cosmos* at the airport. I read about two pages, then put the book down on my seat and went to the plane's lavatory. When I returned to my seat, the book was gone. I realize that a fellow passenger could have taken it. Still, I can't help wondering if my Heavenly mentors, determined to keep a clear channel for A.D., could either have prompted the theft or have simply taken it away themselves, since we know that moving objects seems to be no problem for them.

My other telekinetic experiences cannot be so easily attributed to physical causes. Most of them were caused by my husband, Hal, and all of them have reinforced my faith and my belief in survival after death.

Hal died of congestive heart failure on January 11, 1989. About two weeks later, I got up one morning to find the bathroom lights on. (I am always careful to turn off lights to conserve electricity, but Hal often forgot to turn them off when he got up at night.) As I reached for the light switch that morning, I paused. Perhaps this was a signal from Hal. I shook my head. Maybe I had gotten up during the night and forgotten to turn off the lights. Still, knowing my usual habits, I felt it was unlikely.

I shrugged, switched off the lights, and went downstairs. As I do every morning, I walked directly from the stairs to the front door to turn off the security system. It was already off. I have to admit that I am almost fanatic about activating that system before I go to bed. Now I stood there staring at it, my hand again paused in midair. Had I forgotten to turn it on last night? I smiled, remembering how Hal used to tease me about the way I always double-checked to be sure it was on. It seemed so unlikely that I had forgotten, but how could I be sure? Certainly it was the only logical explanation.

As usual, my next stop was the radio. I always turn it on after disarming the security system. I keep it tuned to my favorite FM station, which plays pleasant, soothing music (my kids call it "elevator music") while I work. When I turned the radio on that morning, though, I got a real wake-up call. I was nearly swept off my feet by a blast of hard rock! I checked the dial. It was set on the hard-rock station Hal always switched to at noon to hear the news report. Sometimes he'd forget to switch back to our favorite station afterward, and when I'd remind him, he'd always apologize and quickly tune it in. Not once since Hal died had I turned on that hard-rock station.

Smiling with relief and joy, I returned the dial to its usual place. The mysteries of the morning were solved. Only Hal would have set the radio dial on that particular station. And it was Hal who had switched the bathroom lights on and the security system off. I was convinced of it. It was his way of reassuring me that he was indeed alive and well in the life beyond.

I sensed on that January morning that this was only the beginning. The time would come when Hal would be able to contact me in a more meaningful way. I was right. When he had adjusted to living on the astral plane, he made contact with me to tell me about some of his experiences there. I know it was Hal, because I sensed the nuances of his personality and also because he mentioned several very evidential things.

He spoke of musician friends who had died and were now with him and forming bands so that they could play together. For many years, Hal had been a professional musician. He had played with some prominent jazz groups and other ensembles of the big band era. After he became a radio and television producer, he continued to play the double bass as a hobby, first with the Westchester Symphony in New York, and later with the Community Orchestra of the Portland Symphony.

He also mentioned bringing "The Kid," his nickname for his beloved Voigt and Geiger double bass, into being. Having it, he said, made him feel that he was truly in Heaven. That double bass was almost a part of him when he was on earth, and I think he regretted leaving it almost as much as leaving his family. I had been given special instructions for seeing that it got into good hands when he was gone.

In addition to being a fine musician, Hal was a composer and an arranger for a number of the bands he played with. He also composed music for some of the radio commercials he produced for a large advertising agency in New York, and he won a "World's Best" international award for one. He says he is now composing music to be used in healing centers on the astral plane.

Evidently it's not all work and no fun where he is now. There is also a great deal of laughter, Hal says, and he still appreciates a good joke and finds a humorous twist to many things. This is very evidential. Hal had a wonderful sense of humor, and he produced many funny commercials that received international awards.

Our family had four delightful dogs over the years—Vickie, Mollie, Mandy, and Candy. Hal mentions playing with them when he isn't involved with other activities. He also speaks of being with Edward, Margaret's husband, who died a few months before him. On earth they had both enjoyed working on inventions, and it seems that they still do.

His message, which follows after the bullets below, brought me much comfort and reassurance.

• • •

Ruth, I'll try to give you a picture of these realms from my own perspective, and it will differ a bit from A.D.'s account. My areas of activity are different from his, and I think people might also like to know what I, as a musician, am experiencing here.

It's been a great joy to find old friends such as George Barnes, Bud Freeman, Norm Schroeder, and others, and we get up wonderful jazz groups together. People who were jazz enthusiasts on earth come to hear us play, and there is a great sense of happiness and comradeship in our gatherings.

Without too much difficulty, through the power of thought, I created "The Kid," and I can tell you it was probably one of my greatest rewards here. I truly felt I was in Heaven when that double bass came into being. Our tables, chairs, and other objects are as solid to us as yours are to you on the physical plane. The vibrations of our created objects here correspond to our own vibrations, so we experience solidity when using those objects, just as you do on earth.

I haven't confined myself to jazz music. There are small groups here who perform in hospitals and healing centers. The music we play there produces vibrations that heal both the astral body and emotions. This is a very special use of music here, and one I am trying to learn more about.

I have also been doing some composing. I learn what symptoms need to be treated, then compose music to use for specific "illnesses" or needs. This area is so extensive that I could spend my whole Hal incarnation here being involved in it.

I'm also, for sheer inspiration and enjoyment, playing a lot of classical music. The symphony orchestras we can join are indescribable. Every instrument ever used by man is part of the magnificent sound produced. The Valley of Praise is where we go to participate in this type of music, and there are always great audiences to hear us. Their response to our playing generates enormous energy, and, in a sense, it seems as if the whole universe reverberates with the sound from there.

All is not serious up here. There is much joy and laughter, and I haven't lost my sense of humor. I can still appreciate a good joke and a funny twist to many things.

I'm frequently close to you on your level, and I'm still helping you in many ways. I know you're aware of this, but I'm not around you all the time. When I'm not, I'm usually enjoying music, playing with our dogs, or participating with Edward in our inventions. Edward and I are studying how to manipulate our "matter" here to interact on your more dense plane. This is a big challenge, and we've had a great deal of enjoyment from studying and experimenting in these areas.

. . .

Margaret's husband, Edward, died in August 1988. Edward had skills as an inventor, and while serving in the Royal Air Force during World War II, he had helped to develop Britain's radar system. He and Hal were good friends, and they were linked by their creativity and sense of humor. Inventing was one of Hal's hobbies, and the three patents he held were proof of his own success in the field. When the two of them got together in the Beyond and decided to convince Margaret and me that they were indeed around, we were in for some big surprises.

They pulled off their first joint caper in July 1991. Margaret was visiting me, and we decided to take a trip on the *Scotia Prince*, the ferry from Portland to Yarmouth, Nova Scotia. At about ten P.M. on July 16th, the night before we were to leave, we went to a supermarket to buy a few things for our trip. It was a clear, moonlit night, and I drove Hal's light-blue station wagon to the store. I'd just had it hand waxed and thoroughly cleaned inside and out. Parked under a bright light in the parking lot, it looked almost new, and I felt really pleased that I'd had the work done.

When Margaret and I finished our shopping and returned to the car, we were appalled. A broad streak of black paint had been sprayed from the rear window down all along the fender on the left side of the car, and from the hood down to the fender on the driver's side. I was furious at the unknown barbarian, and alarmed at what it would cost to repair the damage. Our trip was forgotten for the moment. The vandalism was all Margaret and I could talk about on the drive home.

Still fuming, I opened the garage door with the electric opener, drove into the garage, and got out on the driver's side to examine the mess I'd seen—and found it gone!

Margaret and I were stunned, and immediately suspected Hal and Edward. We couldn't conceive of how they had managed their innocent mischief, and we were still wondering about it on the ship the following afternoon. Then, while we were sitting in a small lounge outside the ship's dining room, Hal suddenly made contact with Margaret. He told us that it was indeed Edward and he who had "painted" the car to give us a sign of their abilities to make an impression on the physical world.

"It took us two years of hard thinking to figure out exactly how we can manipulate the etheric forces to bring our visible matter on the astral plane into a more concrete form that you can see with your physical eyes," Hal said. "We thought that if we here can provide a thought form to assist pioneer scientists, then we can use the same laws to bring a sign to you. What you saw was a thought form, not an illusion. We made black tinted molecules of the pattern of black enamel paint. Having created and deposited it, we could just as easily break it down, and—presto!—it went back into the ether as the molecules it was created from. The energy produced by your anger actually helped us remove the particles. We promise not do this again. Once is enough. We're sorry you were upset, but we hope you appreciate our efforts."

Margaret and I still don't understand exactly what happened or how they managed it. Margaret has asked a number of parapsychologists for an explanation, but we haven't gotten one. Perhaps Hal's explanation to us is as close as we'll come. Margaret says that in all her years of psychic work she has never experienced anything quite like it. We do know what we saw and what we didn't see, and we're sure that Hal and Edward were responsible.

That was the first time Hal and Edward played a trick on us to reassure us that they are around, but it wasn't the last. At least the next time they thought ahead and put us on our guard. That was in 1993. Margaret arrived in South Portland for a visit on October 14th, and Hal and Edward sent a message through to her that they had prepared some more surprises for us, but nothing as shocking as the black paint on the car.

The next morning I went downstairs to find that the security system had been turned off. Later, when Margaret and I went down to the garage to get into my car, her door was locked on the passenger side. I went around to the driver's side, and my door was locked too. I never lock the car doors when the car is in the garage! We remarked about the security system and the locked doors, and Hal came through to

Margaret with this message: "Wait until Sunday and see what we've planned. You're in for a big surprise!"

That Sunday, as Margaret and I got ready for church, I decided to wear a delicate heart-shaped diamond and sapphire ring I had received for my birthday. I was opening its velvet box when Margaret came down the stairs and paused above me. She watched me take out the new ring and hurriedly put my engagement and wedding rings and Hal's wedding band, all three of which I usually wear on the third finger of my left hand, into the velvet box. She saw me place the new ring on my finger and return the velvet box to the cabinet where I keep it.

When we returned from church, I took the velvet box out of the cabinet to retrieve my three rings and return the new one. The box was empty! Margaret and I both remember my placing the three rings in that box and putting it back in the cabinet before we left for church. That's what I always do when I change the rings I'm wearing.

The rings were nowhere to be seen downstairs, and we rushed upstairs to search for them. There, in my jewelry box where I usually keep them at night, I found them. They weren't exactly how I usually place them, but there they were. Margaret and I were both impressed. Except for the paint on the car, we had never experienced anything like it. Hal and Edward were right: on Sunday they had carried out another surprising experiment.

But they weren't finished yet! Later that afternoon Margaret settled down to read in the living room and I went to check a few things in my office. Suddenly, Margaret called me to come quickly. I hurried in to find the floor lamp by my reading chair flashing off and on. When Margaret walked away from the chair, the light would go off. When she approached the chair, it would go on. When I came into the room, it started to flash like a Morse code signal. That *had* to be Edward and Hal. Both knew the Morse code, and Hal had often greeted the *Scotia Prince* in code with our backyard light as it passed through the shipping channel behind our house.

On Margaret's most recent visit, in May 1996, the guys were at it again. From the beginning it had been clear that neither had lost his sense of humor, and their delight in practical jokes was evident in a very olfactory way on Sunday, May 5th. Margaret and I were on our way to church, and when we got into the car in the garage, we thought the car had a very strange odor. We were in a hurry, so I didn't stop to investigate. Besides, I thought that leaving the car out in the air might take care of the problem.

The car stood out in the sun for quite some time during the day while Margaret and I were in church and then visiting with friends. The airing didn't help. By the time we got into it that evening, the odor was indescribably horrible. Now I had to investigate. Between the two front bucket seats I found a plastic bag containing part of a cucumber, which by that time was absolutely rotten. Two days earlier, I had found that piece of cucumber, with signs of spoiling, in my refrigerator. I had put it in the plastic bag and taken it down to the garbage can, which stood near my car in the garage. Edward and Hal knew that the unpleasant odor would attract our attention and let us know that they were again about and playing tricks on us. We laughed, but we both hope that the next time they want to get our attention in the car they'll hide a perfume bottle!

Margaret and I can't offer any of the above accounts as absolute and guaranteed *proofs* of survival after death, but these experiences enhanced our own faith that Hal and Edward are alive and well in the Beyond. A.D. didn't feel that Hal and Edward's activities were insignificant "pranks," but rather that they would further reinforce people's belief in survival. For us, these experiences were very meaningful, and we hope that you will find them uplifting and meaningful too.

A WORD ABOUT
PSYCHIC EXPERIENCES

We carry within us the wonders we seek without us....

SIR THOMAS BROWNE

PEOPLE OFTEN ASK me why they don't have the same psychic abilities as Margaret. My answer is that while most of us can run, few of us have the capability of Olympic gold medalist Joan Benoit. Margaret is a born Joan Benoit of the psychic world. Each of us has the same potential within us, but it is developed to varying degrees.

Throughout his communications, A.D. has stressed that spiritual growth is the purpose of our incarnation on earth. I firmly believe that we can best achieve that goal by staying "grounded." We can be aware that the psychic realms exist and that they interact with our world, but our central purpose in life should be spiritual growth through striving to live by the precepts of God's Kingdom. Psychic experiences and insights are not necessary to accomplish that. Margaret, with all her many given gifts, emphasizes the need to stay grounded. God's presence manifests itself to each of us differently. Some people may *never* have a psychic experience in their entire lifetime, but they may be very highly developed spiritually simply through a deep and abiding inner faith and insight.

Just as there are negative influences and people here on earth, there are negative entities in the lowest astral realm beyond. These entities often harbor an active desire to participate in and influence earth-plane activities. If psychic insight is sought in and of itself without spiritual intent, such as through drugs, Ouija boards, or automatic writing which allows an entity to take control of the writing arm, grave harm can come to the seeker. He or she can become controlled or even taken over by a negative force from the lowest astral realm. In addition, contacts with people involved in negative psychic practices or black magic can be extremely dangerous, producing a harmful impact on the seeker's own psyche.

Safe seeking can be accomplished through meditation and prayer, and by trying to live by the laws our Creator has laid down. Sincere spiritual seekers may then, on occasion, have totally unexpected psychic experiences, which can contribute to their faith and spiritual growth. Those who seek insights through the help of a clairvoyant or psychic should do so with extreme care, and approach only persons of impeccable reputation who are known to have a spiritual and positive intent for the work they do, and whose abilities are recognized by accredited researchers in parapsychology.

I have been blessed in my friendship with Margaret, for she has been instrumental in helping my loved ones reach out to me from the Beyond. And, though I have never sought them, I have been fortunate to have had some insightful and inspiring psychic experiences at various times in my life. They have ranged from an out-of-body experience to a wondrous vision, and each time they have contributed to my spiritual growth.

Sometimes we have an extraordinary experience and, though it helps us grow spiritually, we can't be sure why it was sent to us and we may not realize its purpose until years later. My brother, Al, told me about having an out-of-body experience during his senior year at Augustana College in Rock Island, Illinois.

At the time, he was preparing to attend Augustana Theological Seminary, where our father was teaching. The seminary was located on a hill near the campus, and during breaks in his college schedule, Al would often go up to A.D.'s office in the seminary building to study or read. One morning while he was there reading E. Stanley Jones's book *Victorious Living*, he suddenly found himself out of his body and high up in the sky, as if in an airplane. He could see his body still sitting in A.D.'s office, even though he himself was far removed.

This experience continued for quite a while, and Al suddenly realized that it must be time for his next class. Although he himself remained up in the sky when that thought entered his mind, he saw his physical body, as if by remote control, get up out of the chair, leave A.D.'s office, and walk out of the seminary building and down several flights of stairs to the campus below. At the door of the Old Main Building, where his next class was held, Al suddenly found himself back in his body. He was astounded by what had happened.

Al had been interested in paranormal phenomena for a long time, but he'd never before experienced anything like this. He decided to see if he could repeat the experience by sitting in A.D.'s office at the same time of day and again reading *Victorious Living*. Nothing happened, which is one of the frustrating things about paranormal investigation.

As far as I know, Al never again had an out-of-body experience. We can't be sure why he had even that one, but perhaps it was to imbue him with a personal knowledge of the spiritual self within, which is distinct from the physical body. Surely it served to deepen the faith of a young man who had chosen to enter the ministry. Another possible reason would not come to light until some years later, when Al was Lutheran campus pastor at the University of Montana. A student who was distraught over frequent and unexpected out-of-body experiences turned to him for counseling. Confused and desperate, the student feared that he was going mad. Because he'd had that one experience in A.D.'s office, Al could relate to this student and assure him that he wasn't losing his mind. Through meditation and prayer, Al and the student asked that these experiences cease. They did, and from then on the student was able to lead a normal life.

My own out-of-body experience was quite different. It happened when I was sixteen and very ill with scarlet fever, but it remains fresh and vivid in my memory. During my illness, I had an extremely high fever, and one day I felt very faint. Suddenly I found myself up near the ceiling of the room looking down on my body below. It lasted only a short time, and then I found myself back in my physical body. While I was up near the ceiling, though, I was not aware of the support of any kind of body. Yet I was aware that I was *me* and that I could look down on my physical self below, and I could hear sounds too. So now when A.D. tells us about sometimes being bodiless in a "light of vibrating particles," I can understand what he means.

That one extraordinary experience left me with a deep sense of and belief in the survival of our spiritual self, even when separated from our physical body. More than anything else, it has opened me to the whole, vast field of paranormal study.

There are different types of dreams. Some undoubtedly come from our subconscious mind. Others, A.D. points out, are waking memories of experiences we have when our spirit visits the astral plane while our physical body sleeps. Through such experiences we can be taught something or warned of impending danger.

In May 1995, Margaret and I planned a weekend trip to Bar Harbor, Maine. I decided to drive Hal's station wagon, because it was larger and more comfortable than my own car. I'd recently had the station wagon in for a state inspection, and everything passed in good order. However, about two weeks before our trip, I had a vivid dream. Hal was sitting beside me, and I was driving his car. When I tried to apply the brakes, they wouldn't work. I tried frantically to stop the car, but couldn't. We were speeding down a steep incline and heading straight toward a sheer cliff when I suddenly woke with a start.

The dream was very real, and I was so shaken by it that I took the car to my mechanic the next day. I asked him to pull the wheels and check the brakes. He found that I needed new brake pads on both front wheels, and that the rear wheel brakes needed regrinding. The brakes were repaired, and Margaret and I went on our trip to Bar Harbor with a sense of security.

I get a chill when I think of what might have happened if I hadn't had that dream. Margaret and I would have been risking our lives as we drove down Cadillac Mountain. In a later sitting with Margaret, Hal confirmed that he had been with me in the car on the astral plane to warn me about the brakes, and that I had recalled the astral experience as a dream.

After that experience, I'm more convinced than ever that we need to pay attention to our dreams. I think it's a good idea to keep a journal of them. The meaning of a dream may not be immediately apparent, but we may discover its importance at a later date.

I have been clairvoyant only once. I've never seen A.D. in this way—I have only sensed his presence. Nor have I ever seen Hal or Al, though I've sensed both of them. It was my mother I saw that one time, and it happened the summer before A.D. died.

I had arrived at A.D.'s cabin that evening for a ten-day visit. It was a long trip by plane and bus and car, and I was so tired that I went to bed almost immediately. My bed faced the guest-room door, and shortly after I lay down, I looked up and found my mother, who had died ten years before, standing in the doorway. She was dressed in a navy blue and white dotted-swiss dress like one my daughter, Lynne, had lost. The dress had been one of Lynne's favorites, and we couldn't find it anywhere. I had given up trying. My mother stood in the doorway looking at me for several minutes, and then she vanished suddenly.

I was a bit overwhelmed by the experience. Then I began to realize that my practical mother (remember the china dishes?) had come to tell me that the dress was still around and to continue the search when I got home. Back in New York ten days later, I looked in one of the garment bags in Lynne's closet. The dress had fallen off a hanger and was in a crumpled heap at the bottom of the bag.

I'm grateful that I was given the gift of clairvoyance that one time, further affirming to me that my dear mother is still aware of what goes on in my life.

The next psychic experience I had is very precious to me and can only be described as a vision. It occurred on October 14, 1970, as I was flying from New York to Minneapolis to be at my father's bedside. A.D. had been stricken with a ruptured aneurysm and was gravely ill. When the plane left New York that chilly autumn morning, there was a heavy haze from pollution over the city. Although less dense than over New York, that atmospheric condition continued all through the flight. The ground below was visible, but a misty haze hung over everything.

As the plane approached Minneapolis, I looked down on the Mississippi River winding like a ribbon below us, and suddenly the entire river became a spectrum of the most beautiful, brilliant colors—more beautiful than anything I'd ever seen before. The colors were exquisitely vibrant and unlike any on earth. This breathtaking rainbow was repeated over and over again all along the river, as far as I could see. Gold sparkles overshot the whole, as though a heavenly hand had dusted gold sprinkles all along the river. At the same time, vibrant bands of turquoise and jade green alternated in a huge fan formation in the sky. This was a spectacular sight if there ever was one, and yet no one else in the plane seemed to be aware of it. The other passengers were just sitting there and looking dully out the windows.

The minute the plane touched down, the bands in the sky disappeared. Deep inside me, I *knew* that I had been given a sign. A.D. was going to die, but he would be going to a place far more glorious than any of us can imagine. That beautiful vision was the comfort I received in advance.

A.D. died five days later. Life's journey had ended. Heaven's journey had begun.

NOTES

1. The Reverend Eric J. Gustavson, Sr., Spring Park, MN. Quoted with permission.
2. A.D. Mattson, *Christian Social Consciousness* (Rock Island, IL: Augustana Book Concern, 1953), pp. 106–107.
3. From the funeral sermon preached by the Reverend Allen C. Nelson, St. John's Lutheran Church, Rock Island, IL, October 23, 1970. Quoted with permission.
4. Obituary of Constant Johnson, *The Lutheran*, Vol. X (April 1972), p. 43.
5. Letter to Ruth Mattson Taylor, October 6, 1973.
6. *Witness from Beyond*, ed. Ruth Mattson Taylor (South Portland, ME: Foreword Books, 1980), pp. 15–20.
7. Ibid., pp. 20–21.
8. The exception is clairvoyants, who on occasion will report seeing "nature people"—gnomes and fairies from the astral realm. Margaret, for example, has sometimes seen an astral gnome beneath the big blue spruce tree near my home.
9. "As they were coming down the mountain, Jesus instructed them, 'Don't tell anyone what you have seen, until the Son of Man has been raised from the dead.'

   "The disciples asked him, 'Why then do the teachers of the law say that Elijah must come first?'

   "Jesus replied, 'To be sure, Elijah has already come, and they did not recognize him, but have done to him everything they wished. In the same way, the Son of Man is going to suffer at their hands.' Then the disciples understood that he was talking to them about John the Baptist."
   Matthew 17:9–13

   "Jesus and his disciples went on to the villages around Caesarea Philippi. On the way he asked them, 'Who do people say I am?'

"They replied, 'Some say John the Baptist; others say Elijah; and still others, one of the prophets.'

"'But what about you?' he asked. 'Who do you say I am?'

Mark 8:27–29

"And they asked him, 'Why do the teachers of the law say that Elijah must come first?'

"Jesus replied, 'To be sure, Elijah does come first, and restores all things. Why then is it written that the Son of Man must suffer much and be rejected? But I tell you, Elijah has come, and they have done to him everything they wished, just as it is written about him.'" Mark 9:11–13

"As he went along, he saw a man blind from birth. His disciples asked him, 'Rabbi, who sinned, this man or his parents, that he was born blind?'

"'Neither this man nor his parents sinned,' said Jesus, 'but this happened so that the work of God might be displayed in this life.'"

John 9:1–3

10. "And the Lord asked me, 'What do you see, Amos?'

"'A plumb line,' I replied.

"Then the Lord said, 'Look, I am setting a plumb line among my people Israel; I will spare them no longer.'" Amos 7:8.

11. Margaret, who also has gifts of healing, has been able to heal such tears in the etheric web when she has discovered them through clairvoyant diagnosis. Several years ago, a musician sought her help in desperation. He had been feeling so depleted and exhausted that he could barely function. He was so weak that he could no longer play his wind instrument and he'd had to give up mountain climbing, which was his hobby. Medical doctors had not been able to help him. Margaret's clairvoyance enabled her to see a diagonal tear in the etheric web across his chest. His energy was escaping through that tear. We don't know what caused the rent in his etheric web, but, whatever the cause, it had incapacitated him. After several healing sessions with Margaret, he had a complete closure of the tear and a complete recovery. He was then able to resume his life's activities.

12. J. B. Rhine, *New World of the Mind* (New York: William Sloan Associates, 1953), pp. 33–36. Reprinted with permission of Dr. Sally Feather, the Rhine Research Center.

GLOSSARY

The following words and terms associated with parapsychology are used throughout this book. All have been defined at first use, but readers unfamiliar with them may want to refresh their memory occasionally by referring to the simple definitions provided below.

ASTRAL: Belonging to the world of existence beyond the physical world, a world of finer vibration and sensibility than the physical world.

ASTRAL PLANE OR WORLD: The first level of existence experienced after physical death.

AURA: A distinctive emanation of light energy and color surrounding living things. Although invisible to most people, auras can be seen by clairvoyants, who can often diagnose illnesses by the colors they are able to perceive.

CLAIRVOYANT: A person able to see people, objects, and souls that are not physically present, including people who have died, who may be seen in their surroundings on the invisible planes. Such ability is referred to as CLAIRVOYANCE.

DISCARNATE: A soul or souls who have died and are now living on the invisible planes.

DOORKEEPER: A soul from the astral realm who commits to being a constant guide and protector for an incarnating soul throughout that incarnation. The doorkeeper remains on and exerts his or her influence from the astral plane.

ETHERIC WEB: A protective sheath between the physical and spiritual body. It allows the current personality of an incarnate person to function in a cohesive and integrative way, without intrusion from memories of former incarnations, which are imprinted on the spiritual self.

EVIDENTIAL MATERIAL: Verifiable statements made by a discarnate person when communicating to someone on earth. These statements convince the living person that the communicator from Beyond is indeed the person he or she claims to be. For example, the communicator can, through a medium, give details about his or her life on earth that only the living person seeking contact could possibly know. Such material is often referred to simply as EVIDENTIAL.

INCARNATE: A soul living in the physical body on the earth plane. Until we die, we are all incarnate souls. Since all persons, living or dead, are also souls, the words *person* and *soul* are used interchangeably with the terms INCARNATE and DISCARNATE (see above).

MEDIUM: A person who receives messages from the world beyond. The receiver may or may not be CLAIRVOYANT (see above). He or she may just be psychically sensitive to nonphysical forces, or may receive information mind-to-mind, as in telepathic communication.

PARANORMAL: An event or perception considered to be supernatural. Such occurrences are beyond the realm of ordinary experience and the five senses, and they cannot be explained scientifically.

PARAPSYCHOLOGY: The study of paranormal phenomena.

PARAPSYCHOLOGIST: One who applies scientific methods in studying parapsychology.

PSYCHIC: A person sensitive to nonphysical forces, such as a psychic medium.

PSYCHOMETRY: Clairvoyance in which an object belonging to a person is held by the psychic to aid the clairvoyant process.

TELEKINESIS: Movement of physical objects on the earth plane using mind power. This can be movement accomplished by incarnate or discarnate souls, and it is referred to as TELEKINETIC.

TELEPATHY: Mind-to-mind communication between two incarnate people. Distance seems to be no barrier to such communication.

BIBLIOGRAPHY
AND SUGGESTED READING

This bibliography is suggested for readers who would like to learn more about the paranormal. It lists but a sample of the many books relating to this field of study.

ALTEA, ROSEMARY. *The Eagle and the Rose.* New York: Warner Books, 1995.

BACH, MARCUS. *The Power of Perception.* Marina Del Rey, CA: DeVorss, 1983.

CAYCE, EDGAR. *Auras: An Essay on the Meaning of Colors.* Virginia Beach: ARE Press, 1973.

CAYCE, EDGAR, and HUGH L. *God's Other Door & the Continuity of Life.* Virginia Beach: ARE Press, 1977.

CROOKHALL, ROBERT D. *The Supreme Adventure: Analyses of Psychic Communications.* London: James Clarke, 1961.

GUGGENHEIM, BILL and JUDY. *Hello from Heaven!.* New York: Bantam Books, 1996.

HUMANN, HARVEY. *Death Without Fear.* Lawrence, KS: Penthe Publishing, 1992.

INGE, W. R. *Mysticism in Religion.* Westport, CT: Greenwood Publishing Group, 1976.

JAMES, WILLIAM. *The Varieties of Religious Experience.* New York: Random House, 1993.

KELSEY, DENYS and GRANT, JOAN. *Many Lifetimes.* North Stratford, NH: Ayer, 1980.

KILNER, WALTER J. *The Human Aura.* Secaucus, NJ: Citadel Press, 1995.

KÜBLER-ROSS, ELISABETH. *On Death and Dying.* New York: Collier Books, 1993.

LEADBEATER, C. W. *The Chakras*. Wheaton, IL: Theosophical Publishing House, 1972.

LESHAN, LAWRENCE. *The Medium, the Mystic and the Clairvoyant: Toward a General Theory of the Paranormal*. New York: Viking, 1995.

MACGREGOR, GEDDES. *Reincarnation in Christianity*. Wheaton, IL: Theosophical Publishing, 1989.

MARTIN, JOEL and ROMANOWSKI, PATRICIA. *We Don't Die*. New York: Berkley, 1988.

——. *Our Children Forever: George Anderson's Message from Children on the Other Side*. New York: Berkley, 1994.

MONROE, ROBERT A. *Journeys out of the Body*. New York: Doubleday, 1973.

MOODY, RAYMOND A. *Life After Life*. New York: Bantam, 1988.

——. *Reflections of Life After Life*. New York: Bantam, 1985.

——. *The Light Beyond*. New York: Bantam, 1989.

MURPHY, GARDNER. *Challenge of Psychical Research: A Primer of Parapsychology*. Anshen, Ruth Nanda, ed. *World Perspective Series*, Vol. 16. Westport, CT: Greenwood Publishing Group, 1979.

OSIS, KARLIS. *Deathbed Observations by Physicians and Nurses*. New York: Parapsychology Foundation, 1961.

PURYEAR, ANNE. *Stephen Lives!*. New York: Pocket Books, 1996.

RHINE, JOSEPH B. *New Frontiers of the Mind: The Story of the Duke Experiments*. Westport, CT: Greenwood Publishing Group, 1992.

RING, KENNETH. *Life at Death: A Scientific Investigation of the Near-Death Experience*. New York: William Morrow, 1992.

——. *Omega Project: Near-Death Experiences, UFO Encounters, & Mind at Large*. New York: William Morrow, 1993.

——, and KÜBLER-ROSS, ELISABETH. *Heading Toward Omega: In Search of the Meaning of the Near-Death Experience*. New York: William Morrow, 1985.

STEVENSON, IAN, M.D. *Twenty Cases Suggestive of Reincarnation*. Charlottesville: University Press of Virginia, 1974.

SUGRUE, THOMAS. *There Is a River: The Story of Edgar Cayce*. New York: Time-Life, 1992.

TAYLOR, RUTH MATTSON, ed. *Witness from Beyond*. South Portland, ME: Foreword Books, 1980.

TEILHARD DE CHARDIN, PIERRE. *The Phenomenon of Man*. Trans. by Bernard Wall. San Bernadino, CA: Borgo Press, 1994.

UNDERHILL, EVELYN. *Mysticism*. New York: Doubleday, 1990.